THE ABC OF CLOCHE GARDENING

THE A.B.C. OF
CLOCHE
GARDENING

by

W. E. SHEWELL-COOPER

M.B.E., N.D.H., F.L.S., F.R.S.A., F.R.H.S., Dip. Hort. (Wye)
Fellow of the Agricultural College, Vienna
Director, The Horticultural Educational and Advisory Bureau
and Principal, The Horticultural Training Centre
Lately H. Superintendent, Swanley Horticultural College
Sometime Horticultural Adviser to the Warwickshire and
Cheshire County Councils
Sometime Garden Editor, B.B.C. North Region
Command Horticultural Officer, S.E. and Eastern Commands 1940-48

ENGLISH UNIVERSITIES PRESS LTD.
St. Paul's House, Warwick Square, London, E.C.4

First published 1952

*Made and Printed in Great Britain for the English Universities Press, Ltd., London,
by C. Tinling & Co. Ltd., Liverpool, London and Prescot*

AUTHOR'S PREFACE

It is a pity that the French term " cloche " was ever applied to this definitely English method of crop production.

Continuous cloches are merely glass tents or barns which fit neatly end to end and cover rows of plants—they act, in fact, as low greenhouses, and instead of taking the plants to the glasshouse, as is normally the case, you take the glasshouse to the plants.

We have proved at the Horticultural Training Centre that continuous cloches make all the difference to soil warmth and therefore to earliness. Thus it is possible to get more crops per year from a piece of ground under cloches than without the use of these glass " covers ".

The latest developments concerning soil warming under cloches are most interesting and prove that, with a little extra soil warmth provided by electricity, more can be done with continuous cloches in the winter than was previously thought possible.

We can therefore honestly recommend continuous cloches to all those who want to increase production at any time!

W. E. SHEWELL-COOPER,

Principal,

The Horticultural Training Centre,

Thaxted,

Essex.

CONTENTS

LINE ILLUSTRATIONS

A*

PLATES

CHAPTER I

THE CONTINUOUS CLOCHE
ITS MAKE-UP AND USES

THE word " cloche " is, of course, a French one, meaning bell. French market-gardeners years ago evolved a glass jar in the shape of a bell, which they used and still use for " hurrying on " plants. With such cloches there is no automatic ventilation, and the cropping has to be planned to fit in with the circular jar.

In 1912, Major L. H. Chase, M.Inst.C.E., seeing the use to which these bell-jars were put, devised and patented a continuous cloche which was an entirely new conception, as it provided for continuous glass protection of plants in rows. The obvious advantage of continuous cloches is that they provide automatic ventilation, and yet give all the protection required. They cover the rows of plants where they are growing and a gardener need not devise any special system of planting to use them. Continuous cloches in fact may be made to fit into the normal gardening operations.

The old-fashioned bell-jar is invariably used over soil that has been treated to produce a hotbed. Immense quantities of horse manure had to be made available for this purpose. To-day horse manure is at a premium, and it is therefore of great value to the gardener to know that the continuous cloche needs no hotbed preparation for its successful functioning.

In Great Britain the chief winter enemy of the gardener is damp. Plants suffer far more from damp than they do from frost. Rock gardeners have known this for a long time, for they protect their plants in the winter by covering them with a sheet of glass held in position a few inches above them. Continuous cloches are, then, of great value in the winter, for

11

not only do they keep out the wet, but several degrees of frost also.

Cloches give ideal protection from wind, not only the icy blasts of the winter but also those drying winds of the summer. The ends of the cloche rows should always be kept closed, to prevent these lengths of miniature glasshouses from becoming draught funnels.

Types of Cloches. There are two main types of cloches—the tent and the barn. These may be of different sizes, as the diagrams show (below and p. 14).

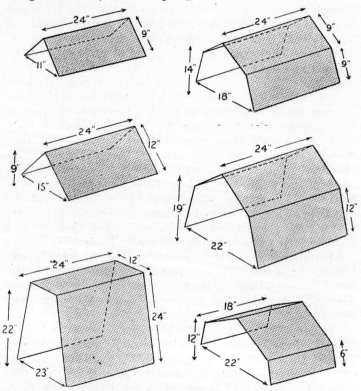

Tent, Barn and Tomato Cloches, showing different sizes.

It will be seen that the tent pattern consists of two sheets of glass held firmly in position by a patented wiring system, while the barn pattern consists of four sheets of glass held in position by four wires bent to a special shape. Because of this special wiring, the cloches are perfectly rigid, and yet the shading the wires produce is reduced to an absolute minimum.

The cloches are very simple to assemble, and can be erected and taken to pieces in a few seconds. As a matter of fact, it seldom proves necessary to take them to pieces once they have been put together, for the keen gardener will find a constant use for them all the year round, and directly they are taken off one row of plants they will go over another.

The various diagrams of the tent-pattern and barn-pattern cloches show exactly how the wires are placed, and it will be seen that the top wire provides an efficient handle for moving these cloches about.

The latest type of cloche is usually known as the tomato " T " or, for convenience, just as the " T " cloche. This, as the drawing shows, consists of three pieces of glass, the top side of which lies almost parallel to the ground. This cloche is 22 inches high and 24 inches long, and it is so arranged that one side can be removed altogether in the summer when it is desired to work among the plants (and this is very useful with tomatoes) without disturbing the rigidity of the cloche at all. It is also possible because a special ring handle is provided to open one side slightly to give extra ventilation— in fact, two ventilation positions are allowed for in this scheme.

The Universality of Continuous Cloches. Cloches are now a necessity and not an extra. They are just as much used by the market-gardener as they are by the home grower. They are excellent in their tens of thousands, covering a large acreage, or in their dozens on the allotment.

At one time, it was thought they would be used almost entirely for vegetables, but to-day they are just as popular with flowers, be they annuals, perennials or bulbs. It was also thought they could have no summer function, but now they are used with great success in the summer months to grow melons and cucumbers, to ripen off onions and shallots,

(a) *The Long Tent Cloche.*

Long tent cloches are best for covering single rows of seedlings or small plants. They are the simplest type of cloche and the lightest to carry about, weighing under 5 lb. each.

(b) *The Long Barn Cloche.*

Long barn cloches use the same size glass as long tents (24 inches by 9 inches), but there are four sheets instead of two. They cover a double row of full-sized lettuce, and are splendid for starting taller crops, peas, beans, runners, sweet-corn, etc., because of extra headroom. With " conversion wires " two long tents can be converted into one long barn.

(c) *The Low Barn Cloche.*

Low barn cloches are wide and squat and are in many ways the best all-round cloche. They will cover five rows of seedlings when used for raising cabbage, Brussels, onion and other plants, or four rows of radish or early carrots or three rows of early turnips or beetroot. They are best for lettuces, and take a double row with plenty of room for an intercrop of peas, onions or carrots.

(d) *Tomato " T " Cloche.*

Tomato " T " is the largest and tallest cloche, and is the best type for growing tomatoes. Owing to its height, it must be pegged down except in very sheltered sites, but this presents no difficulty, for one side of the cloche is movable, and takes out when the plants underneath have to be attended to. During the colder months it is splendid for such crops as broad beans and peas.

Cloches are usually sold by the " set ", which consists of a box of glass weighing about 1½ cwt., and the necessary wires to make up the glass into cloches.

and for taking cuttings of herbaceous flowers and shrubs, and in fact they are the gardeners' daily friend. There is no doubt that further use will be found for them as the months go on.

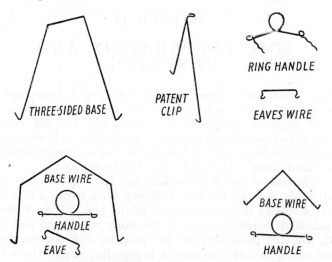

RING HANDLE

THREE-SIDED BASE

PATENT CLIP

EAVES WIRE

BASE WIRE

HANDLE

EAVE

BASE WIRE

HANDLE

Wiring systems for cloches to ensure perfect rigidity.

Movability. Continuous cloches are not cumbersome to move about from place to place, and the minimum amount of time and labour is used for moving cloches if the Strip system as advocated on page 37 is adopted.

CHAPTER II

SOIL PREPARATION AND MANURING

THE experiments carried out at Rothamsted have tended to show that deep cultivation is by no means as necessary as we gardeners thought in years gone by. For soil, therefore, to be covered with continuous cloches it is only necessary to cultivate to a depth of 8 or 9 inches or so, though if there is a hard " pan " below, this should be broken up.

A system of bastard trenching (p. 17) may therefore be advisable, and this consists of digging out a trench 2 ft. wide and a spade's depth at one end of the plot. The soil thus excavated should be taken to the other end of the plot, or the plot may be divided into two portions, as in the diagram, and in this case the soil from A is deposited at just above D. It is necessary, then, to work from A to B and then from C to D, putting the top soil from C into trench B and filling the last trench up with soil provided from A.

When trench A has been made, the gardener should get down into the bottom of it and fork it over deeply, leaving the subsoil where it is. It is in this way that the " pan " is broken up. On top of this forked-up soil should be placed the manure used ; farmyard manure, composted vegetable refuse, finely divided wool shoddy, hop manure and so on, at the rate of one bucketful to the square yard. The soil from A^1 is then put into A^2—that is, on top of the broken-up subsoil and on top of the manure (see diagram, p. 17). By working methodically in this way from one trench to another right through a plot, the ground will be properly cultivated and equally well manured.

This operation is often known as double digging, though

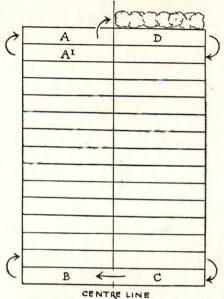

Soil from A put above D
Soil from A¹ put in A
Soil from C put in B
and so on until
Soil from A fills D

SCALE OF FEET

Plan of successful digging scheme.

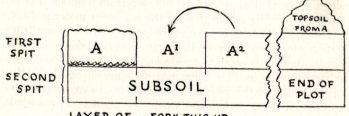

FIRST SPIT

SECOND SPIT

LAYER OF MANURE   FORK THIS UP

Plan of bastard trenching in diagrammatic form. Note the way the manure is placed as a " wodge " in between the sub-soil and soil.

its correct name is bastard trenching. It should be carried out, if possible, in the late autumn or early winter, so that the ground can be left rough and acted on by the frosts and cold winds during the winter. It is in this way that the surface soil becomes aerated and pulverised.

Single Digging. Single digging is carried out during the spring and summer in order to prepare the land for any particular crop. Even in this case it is advisable to dig out a little trench a foot or so wide, and a spade's depth, and to take the soil from such a trench to the other end of the plot. The ground is then dug over trench by trench, finely divided organic matter such as compost being incorporated at the same time if necessary.

Forking. The fork is usually used to help to get the surface soil down to as fine a tilth as possible. A fine tilth is when every particle of soil in the top inch or so is no larger than a grain of wheat. It is impossible to produce this fine tilth if the soil is sticky and wet, and this is where the continuous cloches play their part. They may be put into position a week or fortnight before the seed is to be sown, and thus will not only dry out the soil, but warm it up also, so that the fine tilth necessary for seed-sowing is very easily produced (see Chapter III).

Treading and Raking. Rolling and treading are often done to break up the clods and help to get the soil down fine. The rake is another tool that is used to help to get the soil level and the particles into a sufficiently fine condition.

In stony soils there is no need to try to rake away every single stone that appears. In fact, a certain number of stones are useful, for they help to keep the soil moist underneath.

Hoeing. For some reason or other, amateur gardeners hate hoeing more than anything else, but by using continuous cloches hoeing is reduced to a minimum. The cloches themselves seem to provide their own dust mulch on the surface of the soil, and this prevents moisture from evaporating, and so keeps it down underneath where the plant roots require it. From time to time hoeing under the cloches may be necessary and when it is, short " onion " hoes are usually employed.

Correct Manuring. It is most important, when growing plants under continuous cloches, to see that the soil is enriched with plenty of organic matter ; strawy animal manure or compost should be buried 6 to 8 inches down at the rate of one bucketful to a square yard. Where dung is not available, hop manure may be used, and so may finely divided wool shoddy, seaweed or specially composted vegetable refuse. The great thing is to see that there is a good layer of well-rotted organic matter down below the top spit, and if, when digging, the subsoil is found to be very dry, it is a good plan to soak this layer thoroughly with water before digging over the next spit and covering it.

But in addition to the buried organic matter, it is always advisable when using cloches to fork into the top 2 or 3 inches of soil damped horticultural peat or, if preferred, very finely divided, well-rotted vegetable compost. This gives the little seedlings a good start until they can send their roots down to the bulk of the organic manure below. The peat should be used at half a 2-gallon bucketful to the square yard, and the organic manure at one 2-gallon bucketful to the square yard —as has already been said.

The flavour and food value of vegetables cannot be kept at a high level if the soil is not enriched with organic matter each year. This not only assists in the aeration of the soil and helps to produce a better mechanical and physical condition, but it also provides humus, which has been found to be all important. Organic manures are also valuable for the way in which they assist in liberating plant foods already present in the soil (see *Shewell-Cooper's Guide to Soils and Humus*).

Artificial Manures. In addition to the heavy dressing of organic matter dug in, it will be necessary to add certain quantities of artificial manures ; but even here it is advisable to use those with an organic base. There are several such proprietary manures on the market which should be used at the rate of 5 to 6 ounces to the square yard, and should be applied to the surface of the ground before forking and raking. They can easily be worked in with a rake.

Meat and bone meals and hoof and horn meals are also two

slow-acting manures which contain nitrogen and phosphates and the necessary organic matter. Either of these should be used at 4 ounces to the square yard plus, say, wood ashes at 8 ounces to the square yard.

Soot helps to darken light soils, and so enables them to absorb and retain heat better. It, however, contains nitrogen only, and should be used principally for members of the cabbage family in the spring, at the rate of 5 ounces to the square yard.

In addition to the fertilisers with an organic base, it may be necessary to apply some extra potash, particularly on light soils, and where sulphate of potash is available this should be applied at 1 ounce to the square yard during the seed-bed preparation. Wood ashes are a valuable substitute, especially if fully consumed, and should be used at about $\frac{1}{2}$ lb. to the square yard.

Composting Vegetable Refuse. A very good substitute for dung may be made by the gardener with all the vegetable refuse from the garden, house and allotment. Many experiments have been and are being carried out on this vital and interesting work. But, as a matter of fact, composting is no new method of fertilising the soil. It has been practised for hundreds of years by the Chinese, who are experts at the intensive culture of vegetables.

The John Innes Institute advocates a method of composting which does not include the turning of the heaps. Excellent results have been obtained with the " Indore " method of composting, and in another method a bin is made of old railway sleepers. The material to be composted consists of vegetable refuse, but no hard woody material. When it is filled the heap is treated with a potion of herbs and pure run honey and covered with a large sack. The Bio-dynamic method used by the Rudolph Steiner School also includes the addition of a herbal mixture.

It is impossible to go into details of all the processes, but one which has given excellent results, and has been used at the Horticultural Advisory Bureau for a number of years, is as follows :—

A bin made of wood and covered with a corrugated iron roof is used to hold all the vegetable refuse from the house and garden—potato peelings, tea leaves, dead flowers, rotting leaves, hedge clippings, etc., and litter from the rabbit hutches and poultry runs.

These materials are put in to a depth of 6 inches, and are well trodden. Dried blood is then sprinkled on at the rate of 2 ounces per square yard and watered in, the quantity of water added being controlled by the dampness of the material composted ; it should never be sodden, but thoroughly moist. (Water should not ooze out of the compost when squeezed in the hand.) At every fourth layer hydrated lime should be applied at 2 ounces per square yard instead of the dried blood. Successive layers are made in this manner as material becomes available. At the end of three to six months, depending on the material composted and the time of the year (quicker in spring and summer, slower in winter when the temperature is low), the compost is ripe, being then a dark, black, sweet-smelling substance, containing ample plant foods and providing the necessary " glutinous " physical property for binding the soil particles together. It is possible to use a bottled liquid manure, known as Compospeed, for the purpose. This is applied instead of the dried blood.

The soil is not therefore " blown away " (as has been the case in the Middle West of America, where the dust-bowl arises) ; it provides a medium for the soil bacteria to work upon, and thus plant food is produced in the right condition to be absorbed by the roots and utilised by the plants.

Where no protection is available heaps made in the open surrounded by wire netting are quite successful, but take longer to mature, for the sun dries out the moisture, the winds lower the temperature and heavy rains may give excess moisture. Choose a well-drained, sheltered spot for the heap, digging the soil over first, and, if possible, start with a layer of ripened compost, straw or animal manure. Build in the same way as in the " bin ", or omit the dried blood, relying on the enzymes in the liquid manure to serve as the activator. A dusting of lime should be given for every

6 inches ; a 6-inch thickness of brittle material, such as straw and the dead stems of herbaceous plants, should be sand-wiched, if possible, between layers of fresh green material, such as grass mowings and cabbage leaves. Where a large quantity of green material is to be composted, it should be allowed to wilt a little first, otherwise the water content of the heap may be too high and then an acid slime will be produced, excluding air and retarding the work of the bacteria.

While making the heap, cover with sacks to keep in heat and moisture. Protect if possible from excessive rain, and when the heap is finished a casing of 4 inches of soil may be put on. The heap should be from 10 to 12 feet wide at the base, with sides sloping to 8 feet at the top, and 5 to 6 feet high. The length can be as desired—but it is usually 10 to 12 feet.

Testing for Condition. To test the condition of the com-post, make a hole with a trowel in the side of the heap. If it is slimy, wet and sour-smelling it will be as well to strip off the covering, turn the heap and add drier material and a sprinkling of lime. If it is brittle and smells musty, either add dilute liquid manure or water or, if possible, turn the heap during rain. The compost is ready for use when it has a pleasant, earthy smell and is brownish-black in colour.

Simplicity. Where it proves impossible to make a bin of wood, use wire netting for the sides as already mentioned. This means, of course, that the outside 1-foot strip of material will not be properly composted—but it can easily be cut off when the compost is used and put on the bottom of the new heap.

Remember the general scheme is a 6-inch layer of garden and kitchen waste which if dry must be watered—then the activator, say dried blood, at 2 to 3 ounces to the square yard, followed as soon as possible by another layer of waste material. Repeat the dose until the fourth layer, when you should add the lime instead of the activator. At the fifth layer continue as before.

It is convenient to have the blood (or sulphate of ammonia) in a dustbin with a lid near the heap so that it can easily be used. The lime could be kept in another bin. An " artificial rain " sprinkler on the end of a hose makes it a simple matter to water the heap at any time.

Some gardeners have to use baled straw in which case plenty of water is necessary—it takes 800 to 1,000 gallons to water 1 ton of straw properly.

Lime. It is most important that soils should not be acid, especially as, when continuous cloches are used, more crops per annum can be obtained. Lime sweetens the soil and improves the texture and workability of clays. It adds calcium as a plant food, and as it helps to decompose humus and organic compounds, it releases other plant foods.

Lime should always be applied on the surface of the ground after other manures have been dug or forked in. It is not so important for potatoes and roots as it is for peas, beans and cabbages. Hydrated lime is the simplest to use, and the normal application is 3, 4 or 5 ounces to the square yard, according to the acidity.

Estimating the pH. Scientists have agreed to express the degree of acidity of soil by what, to the outsider, seems a queer notation, *i.e.*, pH 7, which represents the neutral point ; figures less than 7 indicate the degree of acidity and figures more than 7 show the degree of alkalinity. It will therefore be seen that pH 4 is much more acid than pH 6.

The extremes of soil acidity and alkalinity in this country usually vary between pH 8·5 and pH 4·5, and it can be said that most crops do best in soils which range from pH 6 to pH 7·5. Of course, different crops will grow under varying acid or alkaline conditions. For instance, peas and beans seem to like a soil between pH 6 and 7, but potatoes prefer a soil from pH 4·7 to 5·7.

To raise land that you have found to be pH 4 to pH 7 might take 4 tons of lime per acre in the case of sands, and as much as 12 tons per acre in the case of clays, whereas to raise pH 6 to pH 7 takes about 1½ tons of lime per acre in the case of sands, and 3 tons per acre in the case of clays. On the other hand, excess of lime in soils can also cause trouble, and there is what is known as lime-induced chlorosis which is quite

common in the case of fruit trees grown in Kent on chalky
land.

It is possible to test your soil accurately for acidity by
using what is called an indicating fluid. This fluid is green,
but when it comes into contact with the soil it turns red if
the land is very acid, orange if it is less acid, yellow if it is still
less acid and so on. The British Drug Houses offer for sale
a soil indicator which can be bought for about ten shillings and
this enables the home gardener to make soil tests in his garden
or on the allotment in a few minutes.

CHAPTER III

SEED-SOWING, SPACING AND WARMING

THOSE who have not used continuous cloches cannot believe the difference that these glass tents can make to germination, and in consequence to a saving in seed. If the cloches are put into position 10 days or a fortnight before sowing the seed, the soil is warmed and the surface can be got down to an extraordinarily fine tilth.

As the result of this warming and the fine tilth, a much higher percentage of seed germination is experienced. The packet may state that the percentage germination is as high as 80 per cent., but remember that the germination tests are done under ideal conditions in seed-testing laboratories. Given ordinary outdoor conditions, with the cold and the damp, a poor seed-bed, and so on, the germination may easily be reduced to 30 or 40 per cent.

Soil Warming. The value of continuous cloches for warming soil cannot be over-emphasised. By their use seed-sowing is made possible in the winter months of the year. At the Horticultural Training Centre no good results can be *guaranteed* from outside sowings in October, January and February, and yet during these months regular sowings of certain vegetables are made year after year with guaranteed success if continuous cloches are used.

It is of *vital importance*, however, to get the cloches into position 7 to 10 days before sowing. This is not, naturally, so necessary in the summer, but in the winter it makes all the difference to the work.

Electrical Soil Heating. It is possible these days to heat the soil electrically actually under the cloches—a transformer must be bought to reduce the usual voltage to 18 to 20 volts and then galvanised wire can be used as the heating element which is buried 5 inches deep in the soil. Because the voltage is low there is no danger of a shock, neither is there any chance that electric current may be wasted. It is convenient to switch on the electric current in the evening and switch off in the morning, except of course during frosty periods when the heat may be left on all the time. At the Horticultural Training Centre we have discovered that a 20-foot run of barn cloches can be heated for about 1/- a week in the winter, providing the cost of the current is no greater than ¾d. per unit for this work. The temperature of the soil can be increased in this way by say 10 degrees.

The disadvantage of soil warming is that the soil above dries out and therefore we have found it necessary to water the ground under the cloches every 2 or 3 days if the plants are to grow properly. This means a certain amount of cloche moving with consequent extra labour and expense. Northern gardeners, however, may like the idea because with soil heating it is possible to have crops as early as the southerners. Soil heating is often used with cuttings or for forcing chicory, and in fact in some experiments made in the south it was possible to obtain chicory ready for use in salads three weeks after it was planted under whitewashed cloches for this purpose.

The Electrical Propagator. An adaptation of the soil-warming idea has been the introduction of the electrical seed propagator, which consists of two large barn cloches mounted on a specially made asbestos container. The base of the box is filled with horticultural peat which is thoroughly damped beforehand. The zig-zagged galvanised wire is then laid on top of this material and the specially constructed seed boxes sit snugly just on top of the element. They are expressly made of a size so that there are 16 to a propagator.

When the electricity is switched on the transformer does its work and the John Innes Compost in the seed boxes is heated to about 60 deg. F. Many gardeners who have no greenhouse and are completely cloche minded use such a propagator for raising plants of all kinds, and so get a flying

start. Annual flowering plants have been raised in this way
as well as tomatoes, marrows, cucumbers and melons. The
propagator has been used for salad crops like radishes and
mustard and cress and found useful for striking chrysanthemum and dahlia cuttings and for starting off tubers, such as
begonias.

Saving Seed. It always pays to purchase the best seed as
some varieties are better than others, and some seed firms
have specialised in certain vegetables and flowers and have
produced, as a result, exclusive strains. The whole crop
depends on the seed, for if you do not start with good seed,
how can you expect to produce a good crop ?

The best seed may be more expensive, and has a right to
be more expensive, than poor seed ; but as the result of
using continuous cloches, it is possible to make the best seed
go twice or three times as far. Seed under cloches should be
sown extremely thinly. This, of course, results in a vast
economy.

To ensure thin sowing it is a good plan to whiten small
seeds with lime, so that they can be more easily seen. In
cases where vegetables have to be spaced out eventually 4,
5, 6 or 8 inches apart, sow the seed this distance apart, say
three seeds at each " station ". If each of the seeds grows
—as they usually do under cloches—then all that has to be
done is to thin out to one. The sowing of seeds in a continuous line in a drill is a tremendous waste of seed, and
eventually of seedlings.

Quick Germination. The great point about ensuring
quick germination is that plants which germinate quickly
are far less likely to bolt, particularly in the case of endive
and lettuce, than plants which are produced from seed which
germinated slowly.

Market-gardeners are most anxious to ensure immediate
germination in the case of all their seeds, for nothing is more
disheartening than sudden bolting or seeding just when plants
should be ready for use.

Wind Protection. Wind can do a tremendous amount of
harm to plants. Not only does it buffet the leaves and cause

physical injury, but in addition it brings about excessive transpiration with the result that the plants find difficulty in keeping the foliage turgid. This causes a strain on the roots and in due course dries out the soil.

Continuous cloches give the ideal protection against wind, especially those dreadful drying ground winds. The plants are undisturbed, no excessive transpiration takes place and the rate of growth and the " succulence " are therefore increased.

Space Economy. For the small seeds the drills should be very shallow, and for the larger seeds, such as peas and beans, 2 to 3 inches deep. The lighter the soil the deeper the drills should be.

Economise in space by arranging two rows of cloches close together whenever this is possible. A narrow alley-way should then be arranged between the next two rows, and in this way the plants can be tended with very little trouble.

Cloche Moving. When it is necessary to work among or under the cloches, the system adopted should be to move the end cloche of the first row to the other end. The soil may then be stirred and hand-weeding done on the area of ground covered by cloche No. 1. Having done this, cloche No. 2 should be moved forward to where No. 1 stood. The soil that was covered by No. 2 cloche can then be given its treatment, and cloche No. 3 moved forward one place as before. Cloche No. 1 then takes its place at the other end of the row, after all the cloches have been moved up one, as described.

If there are twenty cloches in a line, No. 1 takes the place of No. 20, No. 2 of No. 1, No. 3 of No. 2, and so on. This scheme obviates the necessity of having cloches distributed all over the place while certain weeding or other operations may have to be done.

The Sunny Situation. The function of the cloche is to trap the sunshine—not to manufacture it. Always, therefore, try to have continuous cloches in a sunny situation.

If the rows run east and west, instead of north and south, the minimum amount of shade from the wires is assured and the maximum amount of sun is trapped. Rows that run east and west seem to make the most of the sun late in the afternoon and early evening. Having the continuous cloches, therefore, running in this direction is more important in the winter and early spring than it is in the summer.

Late and Early Sowing. Continuous cloches allow seed-sowing to be carried out both early and late. They are useful when seeds are to be sown in June and July ; with French beans, for instance, the protection they give enables the crop to go on producing tender pods until the end of October. From sowings made in the winter and early in the year, the cloches of course ensure that the crops come into use early, at a time when vegetables and flowers are scarce.

Thinning. It is a great mistake to grow plants too closely under continuous cloches. Thinning, therefore, should be done early, so as to leave the best plants in position at the right distance apart. The root-systems thus have plenty of room for development, as well as the parts of the plant above ground. After thinning, the soil along the rows must be firmed.

It is often economical to thin at two periods, in the first case to half the distances ultimately intended to be left for the crop, and in the second case to remove every other plant. The advantage of this method is that the plants at the second thinning are fit to use in the house and yet do not interfere with the permanent crop.

Intercropping. With the larger cloches it is usually possible to intercrop—to arrange, for instance, that two rows of lettuces are produced on either side of a row of peas ; or to have a row of spring onions sown in between two rows of lettuces. Another scheme is to have two rows of carrots on either side of a row of beetroot, while yet another is to have two rows of turnips on either side of a row of lettuce.

These intercropping schemes are usually carried out with barn cloches, which are wider and so cover more ground. With a little care and ingenuity schemes can be worked out to suit the particular garden or the demands of the individual.

Maturity. The question is often asked, " How long should cloches be left on each crop? " Such a question is not easy to answer arbitrarily, for, naturally, it differs from district to district and from cropping scheme to cropping scheme.

There is no reason at all, providing the cloche is tall enough, why these glass tents should not be left in position over the crops until harvesting time. This is often done in the case of carrots, lettuces, beetroot, spinach, French beans, various flowers and so on. Where, however, the plant reaches the top of the cloche, and starts to press its leaves against the glass, it is time for the glass coverings to be removed altogether and the plant left to grow normally in the open.

Cloches can *start* all crops, and they can also mature most, if desired.

Spacing the Cloches. It may be necessary, especially in warm districts, to space the cloches $\frac{1}{2}$ inch or so apart in order to give extra ventilation during the summer months. The ends of the rows should always be kept closed with sheets of glass or squares of wood or asbestos, especially during the winter and early spring.

Lantern Cloches. Latterly some new cloches have been invented, known as lantern cloches. These are four-sided, being $4\frac{1}{2}$ inches square and $4\frac{1}{2}$ inches high. As they taper slightly towards the top, they nest into one another easily when they have to be stored away. The top of the lantern cloche consists of a little sheet of glass which can either be completely removed or just slid to the side slightly to provide extra ventilation.

The whole object of these lantern cloches is that they can be used for raising plants sown *in situ*. You may want to sow tomatoes, marrows or cucumbers where the plants are to grow (and incidentally this always gives the best results). You may not want to use your big cloches for the purpose, for they are covering other crops, and so you can start off the little seedlings under the lantern cloches, and then, when they have grown too big for this coverage, you can put the taller cloches into position ; by that time they will have been released from the crop which they were covering and forwarding.

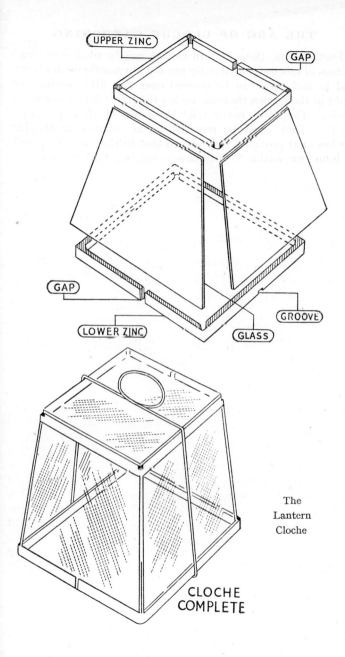

UPPER ZINC

GAP

GAP

LOWER ZINC

GLASS

GROOVE

The
Lantern
Cloche

CLOCHE
COMPLETE

Furthermore, these lantern cloches can be used over small clumps of crocuses, or recently put out chrysanthemum plants, and in fact they can be popped over any little seedling or plant in the garden that one wishes to protect for two or three weeks. They will never take the place of the continuous cloche. They must be regarded as an adjunct to the big cloches, and provided they are treated in that way they will be found invaluable to both flower- and vegetable-growers.

The ideal protectors for Onion seedlings.

Ripening off Tomatoes under Barns. The plants are laid down on peat.

The author's wife instructs the A.T.S. in the use of cloches on a small plot.

Stagshorn Endive under cloches.

CHAPTER IV

CROPPING, CONTINUITY, STANDARDISATION AND IRRIGATION

It is impossible to lay down hard-and-fast rules in regard to cropping, nor would it be advisable to do so. There are some people who feel that continuous cloches should be used only in some special cloche garden devoted to the purpose and this is quite a good idea. The glass tents or barns are, however, invaluable in any part of the vegetable or flower garden. The great secret of their success is that they will fit over any row of plants at any time. They can thus hurry plants along, give protection from rain or frost, warm the soil and even help in the controlling of pests and diseases.

One of the most successful ways in which continuous cloches can be used is for the production of lettuce all the year round. Special hints on the growing of this crop naturally appear in Chapter X, and so it is sufficient here to say that the production of a constant supply of salad crops throughout the winter is one of the functions of cloches that has proved very popular.

As to other crops, they depend greatly on the desires and demands of the garden owner. He may be very keen on tomatoes and so will use a large number of " T " cloches for this purpose. He may be a sweet-corn " fan ", and so will use barn cloches in great numbers to produce these plants much earlier than ordinary outdoor sowings. He knows, in addition, that he can have carrots, peas, beans and so on from 3 to 4 weeks earlier than ordinary outdoor crops.

In order to help beginners who wish to work out cropping schemes to suit their own tastes, charts appear on pages 156–169, where definite times of sowing and times of harvesting are set out. By reading and studying such charts a grower should have little difficulty in working out a plan to suit his particular needs.

Naturally, times vary somewhat from county to county, and there is a great difference between the results that can be obtained in Devon as compared with Northumberland. It is in the north of England, however, and in Scotland that cloches can give the greatest advantage.

Sealing the Ends. Having got the cloches into position, like regiments of soldiers in serried rows, it is always advisable, as has already been said, to close or seal up the ends with squares of wood or sheets of glass. This prevents any possibility of these glass coverings becoming funnels through which tremendous draughts of air are blown. Some cloche firms supply special wires to push into the ground which keep the squares of glass at the ends of the rows firmly in position. Where these are not supplied, bamboos or wooden stakes should be used with the tops securely tied to the handles of the cloches. By closing the ends in this way a low greenhouse is produced covering the plants, with the necessary permanent ventilation assured through the slight opening at the top of each cloche.

It is always better to keep the ends closed the whole time, both in summer and winter. If extra ventilation is needed during the very hottest periods, remove one of the cloches in the line and space the others out an inch or more apart, and so give the extra air that way. Those who have cloches with removable tops may, of course, take these panes of glass out.

Flecking. In very bright sunshine certain plants, *e.g.*, strawberries, cucumbers, aubergines, may need a little protection when ripening their fruits under continuous cloches. The best way of achieving this is to make up a thick paste of lime and water and, with a large brush of the whitewash type, flick a little of the paste on to the outside of the glass to produce a flecked or spotted effect. This breaking up of the sun's rays has the effect of preventing scorching.

Standardisation. I am often asked which is the best type of cloche to get, and this is not an easy question to answer. Personally, I prefer the barn cloche, 24 inches wide, 18 inches high and 24 inches long. The tent cloche, however, which is 14 inches long by 12 inches wide is also a very useful size.

There is a great advantage in having large numbers of cloches of the same size and trying to work to some standard in the garden. This facilitates the transference of cloches from one crop to another, and also makes it much easier to calculate rows, distances and the necessary cloche coverage required.

Each type of cloche has its use—the tomato " T ", for instance, is excellent for tomatoes, while the lantern is first class for raising seedlings.

Continuity. Reference has already been made to the importance of using cloches continuously. They should, in fact, never be out of use. They may be removed from covering one crop that is getting too tall and be transferred immediately to cover another crop that needs their help and protection.

Suggested Continuous Cropping for Vegetables

Spring	Summer	Autumn and Winter
Lettuce	Tomatoes	Lettuce
Carrots	Marrows	Carrots
Turnips	Cucumbers	Endive
Beet	Sweet corn	Salad onions
Peas	Melons	French beans
Runner beans	" Self " blanching	Corn salad
Salad onions	celery	Onions
Radishes		Radishes

Not only should they be used all the time, but they should always be in continuous rows, and experience has shown that the longer the rows, the better. It is useless just to put one cloche over one plant or over part of a row. It is the accumulated effect of the one cloche alongside the other that is so valuable.

Therefore, keep your cloche rows continuous. See that they are straight, and that the cloches fit against one another as closely as possible.

Wrapping. Continuous cloches when stood up on end can be placed around any plants in such a manner as to enclose

them or, to use the modern term, to " wrap " them. Sometimes a complete wrapping is not possible and then the cloches
may be placed on end behind the plants to act as reflectors.
Standing in this way they give protection from wind (a very
important point) and they ensure that the plant receives the
maximum sun heat available.

Irrigation. It is important that the soil should be in the
right condition before putting the cloches into position ; read
the paragraph on correct manuring, page 19, carefully.
Notice the importance of working the damped horticultural
peat into the top 3 or 4 inches, as well as having the layer of
damped (if necessary), well-rotted organic matter below the
top spit. When this has been done correctly cloches may be
put into position, and must not be moved (except under the
direst circumstances) for watering.

If irrigation is necessary, this should be done over the
cloches. The water will then run down the sides of the glass,
seep into the soil and so moisten the roots.

In small areas a channel can be hoed out each side of a row
of cloches and the water poured in these ; but even in small
gardens it is possible to irrigate overhead by means of whirling
Rain King Sprinklers or one of the Brosson types, and the
use of water in this way is not wasteful.

The organic content of the soil must be kept up, and the
ground should be in a sufficiently moist condition before the
cloches are put into place. It may be necessary, for instance,
in the summer to give the ground a good soaking before it is
dug over for cloche culture. *Note.*—Do the soaking before
the ground is dug over, and not after. The moisture gets
down properly if this is done, while if you dig first of all, it
will only wet the top 3 or 4 inches, and incidentally make
the ground like a mud puddle.

The overhead irrigation lines adopted by market-gardeners
are ideal for use in connection with continuous cloches, for
they ensure that an inch or so of artificial rain can be given
at any period during the summer.

CHAPTER V

PLANNING AND STRIP CROPPING

A QUESTION which is often asked is : " What is meant by the word *continuous* ? " Briefly, the answer is : (1) that the cloches are always used adjacent to one another in continuous lines, and (2) that they can be used continuously, that is to say, all the year round. The danger of insisting that the cloches are never out of use is that amateur gardeners tend to move them from one corner of the garden right to the other and thus they waste time and labour, and may easily incur breakages. Therefore, it is necessary to work out some plan which will ensure : (a) that the cloches are in long straight rows, and (b) that they only have to be moved a couple of feet or so the moment their function on the original strip is over.

Cloches, it must be remembered, are mobile ; that is their great feature. They are not like a frame which is usually permanent and in which the crop is housed until it is large enough to be removed. With the cloche, it is the glass that moves on and not the plant. Remember that in the earlier chapters, stress has been laid on the digging in of plenty of organic matter and once the seed has been sown in ideal soil, the plant must be given the chance of developing properly at that spot. It can be provided with a flying start by the warmth and protection that the cloche engenders—it is never coddled, but is grown hardily, and then when the plant gets too tall to be housed in this temporary though miniature glass structure, the cloches move on.

When the Horticultural Training Centre was in Kent we had a definite Cloche Garden for educational and demonstrational purposes, and we soon discovered that the golden rule was to aim at having 1 square yard of really well-manured ground for every 1-foot run of continuous cloches in use.

We started off with a plot 20 feet long and 18 feet wide and used two 20-foot rows of cloches, one starting at one end of the plot and the other at the other end. We arranged that they covered three different crops in the season, 1 foot being allowed in between the positions of each cloche line (see drawing).

The cloches were first in position A, then they were moved on to B and later to C, and we arranged it that the next move would be back to position B again and lastly back once more to strip A. The other set of cloches also worked in towards the centre and back again to the outside in the course of the 12 months. We then found that to have only this minimum area for cloches was too parsimonious because it was always useful to be able to move the cloches on to a position which we may describe as D, even if only for a month or so, while the plants at B were coming to full maturity, and so instead of allowing a strip of land 18 feet wide which is the absolute minimum for two rows of cloches, we developed a strip 30 feet wide giving a little land to spare for any emergency. It can thus be seen that whether the cloche rows are 20 feet or 30 feet long the width of land allowed for the work must always be the same, under this particular system.

The Three-Strip System. What we have already described is really the three-strip system of cloche cropping, but in an attempt to make it appear simple we have shown how we worked out the idea. It is quite possible to explain the three-strip system in a diagrammatic way as seen below, and

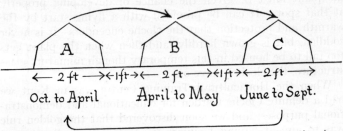

Here we have a chance of seeing the three-strip Rotation in operation. It entails the minimum amount of cloche moving.

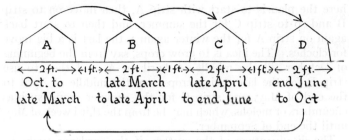

A   B   C   D

←— 2ft. —→←1ft.→←— 2ft. —→←1ft.→←— 2ft. —→←1ft.→←— 2ft. —→

Oct. to   late March   late April   end June

late March   to late April   to end June   to Oct.

This is a better but " more difficult to work out " system. It entails four moves in all and makes the utmost use of cloches with the minimum labour.

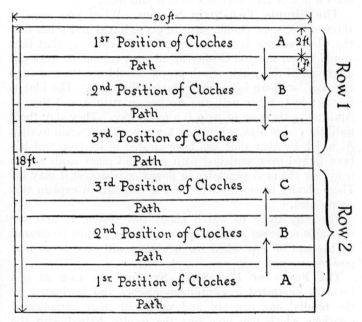

Three-strip method—Working from the outside towards the middle. The Paths are of course only temporary trodden down earth.

here the plan is to start with strip A, then move on to strip B and so to strip C for the summer, and then to start back again on strip A for the winter again ; the last is a big move for cloches.   The idea is to grow crops, say from the beginning of October till the middle of April on A, and then to use strip B for the late spring crops, say the middle of April to the end of May, and strip C for the summer crops, such as cucumbers or melons, which may be from the third week of May until the end of September.

The disadvantage of the system, if the gardener sticks to the same land for cloches each year, is that he tends always to grow the same kind of crops on the same area of land each year ; that is the reason why I previously advised the use of extra ground so that instead of moving back to A, you can start a new A the other side of C if you wish.

The Simple Two-Strip System.   When you mention three strips, some people seem to get agitated and think that the whole scheme is far too complicated—they say that they would rather not use cloches at all than trouble to work out a scheme of this kind.   Such people should use the two-strip rotation for there is nothing simpler than this.   The idea is to start in October with the cloches on strip A and then in April move them on to strip B a foot away.   They stay there until the end of May, when they are moved back again to strip A, which by that time has been cleared of its crop and has been forked over, enriched with peat and plant foods and is ready for the next vegetable or flower or whatever it may be. There should be no need to have a diagram to explain this simple idea.

The only thing to watch about this system is that the vegetable or flower which is grown on strip A must be cleared by the end of May when the new crop will need to go into position.

The Four- or Five-Strip System.   As soon as one becomes interested in continuous cloches and fascinated by the results, one can try and work out more complicated rotations which will give just the results desired with the minimum amount of labour.   Remember that cloches are not only used for flowers, salads and vegetables—they can also play their part, as will be seen in Chapter XIV, in the case of strawberries or raspberries. The more crops that are introduced into the general scheme the more interesting can the idea of strip rotation become. For instance, the strawberries need to be covered from, say, January to the end of May and thus the use of the cloches during that period cuts across the normal times advised for strip rotations.

The great thing is to sit down with some squared paper in winter time and to work out exactly how the cloches are going to be used over the garden devoted to the crops which do best under these miniature greenhouses. It is not worth while, for instance, to include parsnips which do just as well without cloches or Jerusalem artichokes which will yield heavily without any extra help. Use the cloches intelligently and, if you like, make little models of the cloches to scale in wood and actually lay them on the squared paper where they are going to be for the first period, and then move them on until the whole of your four- or five-strip cropping plan has been organised.

Take a typical example (and also study the diagram on page 42). Strip A starts off with lettuce sown in October, and the cloches are moved on late in March to cover the early beet on strip B ; the cloches are moved on to strip C where it is intended to grow, say, French beans or tomatoes ; then, at the end of June when all fear of frost is passed, to strip D where the summer crops will be, such as frame cucumbers or melons. Another move can be made if necessary in September to cover potatoes planted in August, with the idea of digging them at Christmas. This gives us our fifth strip. When, however, the fifth strip is adopted it is difficult to start off again with the normal cropping for strip A, *i.e.*, the lettuces to be covered in October or the spring cabbage which is sometimes covered in the north. But, on the other hand, once the potatoes are dug at Christmas time, it is possible to alter the rotation scheme and start with onion, celery and brassica plant raising in January, and so the general planning of the strip cropping is slightly altered from year to year.

B*

The four- or five-strip system, however, which the diagram shows is not only effective but simple to operate, and on the whole is the best of all the rotational cropping schemes I have planned. The rather more detailed drawing below shows what happens on the cloche land when the miniature greenhouses move onwards.

Four- or Five-Strip System

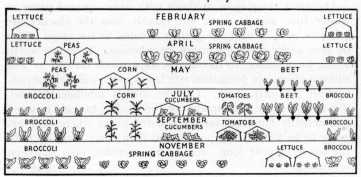

The Four-Strip Rotation, introducing Lanterns. It is possible to get a flying start on some of the strips by introducing what may be called the lantern cloche—this is really an adaptation of the jam jar, which we have used again and again with great success. In 1950, for instance, when we took over our new Training Centre at Thaxted, we sowed literally hundreds of marrows *in situ* under jam jars and the method was extremely successful.

The plan is to start with the broad beans on strip A—these will be sown in October and will be covered until late March. The cloches will then go on to strip B where it is intended to sow annuals for use as cut flowers. The next move is, of course, on to strip C to cover marrows, but it won't be possible to de-cloche the annuals until late April and this will be rather late to start off marrows and so the lantern cloches or jam jars are used upside down to cover the seeds of marrows sown *in situ* about the end of March or the beginning of April. The marrows then grow well and when the cloches are moved from strip B late in April they go over marrows which have developed considerably by that time.

Now we have strip D to bear in mind and once again we want early cucumbers and so we sow some seeds *in situ* again about the beginning of May, and cover with the jam jar or lantern cloche. The plants are then growing well by the beginning of June, when the barn cloches can be removed from strip C to go over the cucumbers on D. The diagram shows how the scheme works in principle.

FOUR STRIP ROTATION

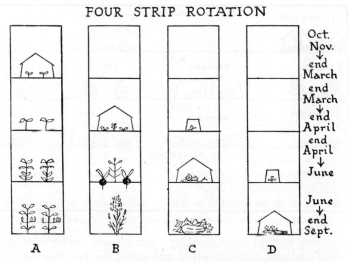

Here is the idea of four-strip Rotations with lantern cloches in diagrammatic form. Note the dates at the end of the chart.

The Double-Cloche Method. It saves time and makes for the maximum efficiency if the strips of land can be of sufficient width to accommodate two rows of cloches running side by side separated only by a 3- or 4-inch width, and under this scheme 18 inches should be left at the side of the pair of cloches instead of a foot as advised for the single-cloche line system. Therefore, there are two rows of cloches 2 feet wide, equalling 4 feet, a 4-inch space in between them and then 18 inches for the pathway. This makes 5 feet 10 inches in all and so 6 feet is usually allowed per strip.

If you adopt the two-course rotation, the scheme is to have a double row of cloches with an adjacent strip of the same width carrying no crop ; then a third strip with a double row of cloches, probably protecting a similar crop to the first strip ; after this a fourth strip bare and so on right across the land to be devoted to cloche growing. The pairs of cloches

The Double Cloche Method

It is always more economical to work cloches in pairs as above.

are very easy to move together—you lift one cloche with one hand and one with the other and move the two together to their new bit of ground. When the crop on the first strip is cleared the land is once again manured and prepared in readiness for the third crop when the pairs of cloches will be moved back to the first strip once more. This is a simple method and there is no doubt that using the two rows of cloches in juxtaposition to one another does save room and time.

Crops and Cloche Periods. Throughout the book, chapter by chapter, details are given as to how the various crops should be grown and suggestions are made as to when the cloches should be used, and therefore it should not take the reader long to work out strip rotations which should suit his own particular needs, but it may be as well to divide up the bulk of the crops into periods of sowing to give pointers which will help with the planning. The four main divisions are : (1) early spring, (2) late spring, (3) summer, and lastly (4) autumn.

Early Spring

List of crops	Harvesting starts
Onion plants	April
Lettuces	April
Peas	May
Turnips	May
Carrots	May
Radishes	March
Beetroot	June
Annuals	May
Spring cabbage	March

Late Spring

French beans	June
Marrows	Mid-June
Sweet corn	July
Tomatoes	July
Runner beans	July
Ridge cucumbers	July

Summer

Frame cucumbers	July
Melons	August
Late tomatoes	August
Aubergines	September
Capsicums	August

Autumn

List of crops	Harvesting starts
Endive	October
Autumn lettuce	November
August-planted potatoes	Christmas
Tomato fruit ripening	Until end of November
Sweet peas	End of May
Annuals	End of May
July-sown peas	October–November
July-sown French beans	October–November

Cloche covering for odd periods. There are a number of crops which don't easily fit into a normal two-, three- or four-strip cropping scheme—gardeners using them must work out special schemes to keep the cloches continually in use.

Crops	Cloches in use	Harvesting starts
Strawberries	January to June	Late May
Violets	Sept. to early March	February
Polyanthus	December to March	February
Asparagus	January to April	Cutting in March
Carnations	May to July	August
Onion ripening	July to August	September
Cauliflower plants	October to November	*March
Cabbage and sprout plants	January to March	*March
Bulbs	When growth shows until stems need extra height	

* These crops are of course next planted out in the open where they are to mature.

CHAPTER VI

ROOT CROPS

ROOT crops are very important, for most of them are rich in Vitamins A, B1, B2 and C.

There is not much point in growing parsnips, swedes or maincrop turnips under continuous cloches, though in the north it has been found worth while to start these root crops under cloches so that the sowing may be done earlier. This is particularly necessary in the case of parsnips. Cloches are, however, ideal for bringing along quick crops of the early types of carrots, turnips and beetroot. They can also be used to start off any root crop, and on occasions are invaluable for kohl-rabi, salsify, scorzonera and Hamburg Parsley.

BEETROOT

The beetroot may be divided roughly into three classes : the round, the tankard and the long beet. In the case of the round beet, two further divisions may be made—the earlies and the main crops.

Continuous cloches are generally used for the earlies, the gardener aiming to produce several crops of roots about the size of a tennis ball, or even smaller. These are pulled purposely while young and fresh, and prove particularly delicious in consequence. Several sowings may thus be made throughout the season.

As mentioned, however, in the introduction, there is no reason at all why continuous cloches should not be used either to warm the strip of land where the seed for main crops is to be sown, or to cover up the rows until such time as the leaves touch the top of the glass tents.

Soils and Manures. The lightest soils suit beetroot best, though they will do well on heavy clays if these are lightened by digging in sand, strawy material, flue-dust, etc., and if the soil is dressed with lime.

Large quantities of fresh farmyard manure should not be dug in, for this causes the roots to fork. Seaweed has proved an excellent manure for beetroot and may be used at one barrowload to 10 square yards. In addition, fork into the top 3 or 4 inches a good fish manure, meat and bone meal or any complete fertiliser with an organic base at 3 or 4 ounces to the square yard. On very sandy soil give salt in addition, at the rate of 2 ounces to the square yard.

Sowing the Seed. Under cloches the first sowing should be made at the end of March or the beginning of April. The roots will thus be ready to use at the beginning of June; one row under large tent cloches, two rows 12 inches apart under low barns.

Sowings may then be made at fortnightly intervals if required, the last sowing being about the second week of July, and the roots being ready, in consequence, in September. These may, if desired, be kept throughout the winter and stored in sand or ashes. The drills should be $1\frac{1}{2}$ inches deep.

Thinning. When the plants are 3 inches high, thin to 4 inches apart, and then, when the roots are the size of golf balls, thin to 8 inches apart. The later thinnings may be eaten.

Transplanting. It is possible to transplant round varieties of beetroot seedlings if this work is done when they are young enough. Good waterings must be given, however, every day until the transplanted beet are well established.

Harvesting. There is no difficulty in pulling the roots grown under cloches. In fact, they are much easier to pull up than those grown out of doors in the normal way. Care should be taken, however, not to bruise them, or bleeding may take place.

Before storing, the leaves should be cut or twisted off an inch above the roots, the leaves thus removed being put on the compost heap to rot down as manure.

Varieties
Early Wonder. An early round type.
Crimson Ball. Good flavour.
Empire Globe. Entirely free from disfiguring white rings.
Cook's Delight. Tankard shape.
Detroit. Fine colour.

CARROTS

Under cloches there is no difficulty in having carrots all the year round. They contain 9 per cent. of carbohydrates and their calorific value stands at 193.

Soils and Manures. Carrots prefer a deep, well-cultivated, sandy loam ; and heavy soils should be improved by adding sandy or gritty material and plenty of horticultural peat. It is better on the clay soils to grow the shorter-rooted types.

Always put the cloches into position a fortnight before sowing the seed, and thus the soil will get down into the fine tilth so necessary for this crop. Fork in lightly a good ferti-liser with an organic base, at the rate of 4 ounces to the square yard. Do not dig in fresh farmyard manure, as this causes the roots to fork.

Sowing the Seed. The drills should be 1 inch deep and about 9 inches apart depending on the type of carrot grown and the cloches used. To ensure specially thin sowing, mix powdery horticultural peat or dry earth with the seed in equal proportions beforehand.

Early types can be sown 5 inches apart—*i.e.*, four rows under low barn cloches.

A good system is to sow a row of carrots in between two rows of lettuce under low barn cloches. Another is to have two rows of carrots on either side of a central row of lettuce. Two rows will fit quite well under the large tent type of cloche, or four rows under the low barns.

The months to sow are January, February, August, September and October.

Thinning. If the sowing has been done properly there should be no need to thin. However, where necessary the plants should be thinned to an inch or so apart in the case of the short varieties, but to 6 inches apart in the case of the main crops.

Transplanting. Carrots may be transplanted when they are very tiny, but they do not transplant well on the whole.

Harvesting. The roots may be pulled as desired and stored in sand or dry earth in a shed, having first cut the tops off.

If cloches are used little storage will be necessary, for even in the depth of winter roots usually pull up quite easily.

Pests. The great pest of carrots is carrot fly, but under cloches the early roots are pulled before the eggs are even laid. With the later sowings the cloches seem to keep the flies away.

Varieties

Primo. For the earliest sowing of the year. Produces small, cylindrical roots.
Early Nantes. An excellent type for cloche work.
Perfect Gem. Similar to Early Gem.
Delicatesse. A particularly delicious type.
Early Market. A good variety for August sowing.
James' Scarlet Intermediate. A first-class variety to sow in February as a main crop.
Red Lady. Excellent under cloches.
Ideal. Good colour and flavour.

TURNIPS

The main function of cloches in connection with turnips is to produce delicious tennis-ball sized roots almost all the year round. In the open the roots have a tendency to run to seed, and are usually badly attacked by the flea-beetle. Under cloches they seldom suffer from either.

Soi's and Manures. The early maturing types of turnips will do well on almost all soils, except those that are very shallow.

Do not manure heavily with farmyard manure, but fork into the top 6 inches horticultural peat at $\frac{1}{2}$ lb. to the square yard, and, in addition, apply a fertiliser with an organic base, such as a good fish manure or a meat and bone meal, at 4 to 5 ounces per square yard.

Sowing the Seed. The first sowing should be made in February, the drills being drawn out $1\frac{1}{2}$ inches deep and 8 to 12 inches apart, depending on the cloches used. Two rows fit quite well under the large tent cloches or three rows under the low barn cloches.

Further sowings may be made each month until the end of July. It is then that the winter turnips should be sown, the drills being 12 inches apart and the seed spaced out, if possible,

9 inches apart. This allows two rows to be sown under the low barn cloches, one under large tent.

Thinning. The plants should be thinned to 6 inches apart when they are an inch high. It is most important in the case of turnips not to allow the leaves of one root to touch the next in the early stages, so thinning must be done early and rigorously. The winter-turnip sowings should be thinned to 6 inches apart when 2 inches high. A further thinning has to be done to 1 foot apart as soon as the roots are fit to use.

Harvesting. The roots should be pulled when they are young and fresh, before they get coarse.

The winter turnips must be kept under cloches throughout the winter, and if the weather should become extraordinarily frosty it may be necessary to cover the cloches with a little straw or bracken. The roots can then be pulled at any time.

Varieties

Model White. Good early variety.
Early White Milan. A pure white.
Jersey Pearl. Heavy cropping, delicious.
Early Snowball. Round and firm.
Long White Forcing. The long shape.

For a winter turnip :
Chirk Castle. Flesh firm and white.

PARSNIPS

Parsnips may be started under cloches if necessary, allowing earlier sowings to be made in the north and also ensuring almost perfect germination. Sow in February. Arrange the rows $1\frac{1}{2}$ feet apart and the plants 9 inches apart in the rows ; sow in drills $1\frac{1}{2}$ inches deep. This means one row per tent cloche row.

Remove the cloches directly the leaves touch the sides.

Varieties

Shallow soils :
Clucas' Intermediate. A heavy cropper.

Deeper soils :
Tender and True. Clearer and smoother skin than other varieties.

SWEDES

Swedes may, like parsnips, be started under cloches to give them a good send-off. Sow the seed in drills 18 inches apart and 1 inch deep ; under cloches sow early in May. This means one row per tent cloche row. Aim to thin out the plants to 1 foot apart. Remove the cloches when the leaves touch the sides.

Varieties

Purple-top Swede.   Roots well shaped, good colour.
Bronze-top Swede.   The best-flavoured variety.

KOHL-RABI

This is similar to turnip, but has a nuttier flavour. Sow early in March, and further sowings may be made every fort-night till the beginning of August. Aim at rows 18 inches or 2 feet apart. Thin the plants to 6 inches apart. Remove the cloches when the plants get too big for them.

Varieties

Earliest White.   Delicately flavoured.   Used for early sowings.
Early Purple.   Used for midsummer sowings.

SALSIFY

Salsify is a delicious, unusual root crop which may be started under continuous cloches. Treat as for carrots. Sow seed early April. Aim at the drills being 1 foot apart and 1 inch deep. Thin to 8 inches apart. Remove the cloches early June.

Variety

Mammoth Sandwich Island.   Excellent flavour.

CHAPTER VII

PEAS AND BEANS

ALL members of the pea and bean family prove excellent crops for growing under cloches. They are valuable because they add nitrogen to the soil, and so leave it in a better condition than when the seed was sown. The ash from the burnt, dried tops of broad beans is very rich in potash.

Runner beans, when sown under cloches, often come into cropping three weeks earlier than ordinary out-of-door sowings. They enable the gardener in the north to sow beans three weeks or a month earlier than he would normally.

BROAD BEANS

Seed sown in January under cloches produces plants which come into cropping quite as early as normal November sowings in the open ground. There is no risk of loss by frost under the glass tents. Also by delaying sowings until January or February the ground can more advantageously be used for such winter crops as lettuce, spinach or radishes.

Soils and Manures. The broad bean is happy on almost any soil.

Farmyard manure or well-composted vegetable refuse should be dug in at the rate of one good barrowload to 10 square yards. In addition, into the top 3 or 4 inches should be forked a ferti-liser with an organic base, such as a good fish manure or meat and bone meal at 5 ounces to the square yard.

Sowing the Seed. Drills should be drawn out 5 inches wide and 3 inches deep, a double row of beans being sown in the drill, zig-zag fashion, so that the seeds are 6 inches apart. After covering over, a large cloche should be put into position, and another row should be sown down the centre of the next cloche row which should be as close as possible to the original one. An alley-way should then be left for the next pair of cloches, and so on. As the tent cloches are not going to be left in position all through the life of the beans, there is no difficulty in having two single rows of broad beans per " large " cloche row.

Make the first sowing in January and further sowings in February and early March. In every case start the beans under cloches, which are removed when the plants are 6 inches high and, if available, taller barn cloches substituted. From the January sowings it should be possible at the end of April to remove the cloches altogether and use them for another crop. A little more space may be left between the cloches during flowering so as to ensure perfect fertilisation.

Two or three beans should be sown at the end of each row, so that, should any gaps appear, the plants that result from these end-of-row sowings can be used for filling up. Broad beans transplant quite well.

General Notes. The earliest broad beans under cloches escape the fly. But with later sowings keep a close watch, and immediately there are any signs of this give a thorough spraying with liquid derris. It is not necessary to pinch out the tops to control black fly.

Harvesting. Pick the pods regularly when young.

Varieties

Aquadulce. A tall-growing variety bearing enormous pods.
Seville Mammoth Long Pod. Bears large, well-filled pods of good flavour.
Giant Windsor. Very excellent flavour.

FRENCH BEANS
(Sometimes called Dwarf or Kidney Beans)

The French bean comes into cropping earlier than its cousin, the runner bean, and withstands drought possibly better than any other vegetable crop.

Soils and Manures. The French bean prefers a light soil to a heavy one.

Prepare the ground as advised for broad beans, and, as lime

is a necessity for all members of this family, after forking in the artificials apply hydrated lime to the surface of the ground, at from 4 to 7 ounces per square yard, depending on the acidity of the soil.

Sowing the Seed. Drills should be prepared as advised for broad beans, 2 inches deep, and the seed spaced out in these 4 inches apart. Rows may vary from 2 to 3 feet apart. It is better on the whole to have one row per cloche row.

The first sowing should be done at the end of March, and from such a sowing under cloches beans will be picked in June. Sowings may be made once a fortnight until July, if necessary. The July sowing produces delicious pods in October.

The rows should first of all be covered with barn cloches, and then, when the plants are well grown, these should be replaced by tomato " T "s or they may be removed altogether.

General Notes. If the weather proves particularly dry, it may be necessary to take out shallow drills on each side of the row of cloches and give these a thorough soaking from time to time. Overhead irrigation is also useful.

In the case of the summer sowings it is possible to leave the pods on and allow them to ripen, when the beans may be shelled out to be stored and used as haricot beans in the winter.

Varieties

The Wonder. Good for early work.
Black Wonder. Useful for summer sowings. Is resistant to halo blight.
Bounteous. Bears medium-sized pods, almost stringless.
Feltham Prolific. A dwarf variety for those with low cloches only.
The Prince. Very good for cloche work.

RUNNER BEANS

Cloches here make all the difference, for they render it possible to sow the seed early without any fear that the young plants will be ruined by frost. Runner beans started in this way are usually three weeks ahead of those grown without this protection.

Soils and Manures. Whatever the soil, it should be

deeply worked, bastard trenching (see page 16) being recommended.

Farmyard manure or properly composted refuse should be dug in at the rate of one good barrowload to 10 square yards. This should be buried below the top 7 or 8 inches of soil. In addition, a fortnight or so before the seed is sown, an organic fertiliser should be forked into the top 3 or 4 inches, at the rate of 4 to 5 ounces to the square yard. Just before seed-sowing, hydrated lime should be applied to the surface of the ground, at 3 to 5 ounces to the square yard.

Sowing the Seed. The seed should be sown in drills as advised for broad beans, being spaced 9 inches apart. The first sowing should be made about the middle of March in the south, though in the north it is better to delay until the second week of April. As a result, beans are ready to use from mid-July onwards, whereas from ordinary outside sowings they do not usually turn in till August.

General Notes. As soon as the plants are ready to climb, the cloches may be removed and stick or string supports arranged for them. Where it is proposed to grow runners on the dwarf system, the tops of the plants should be pinched back when they are 18 inches high, and further pinching back should take place when the subsequent growths are 18 inches long. In this case after the cloches are removed they may be placed on the weather side of the plants to give a certain amount of further protection for a fortnight or so.

Harvesting. Pick the beans regularly when they are ready, and a continuous supply will be assured until the autumn.

Varieties

Princeps. An early variety, particularly suited to cloches. Should always be grown pinched back, *i.e.*, dwarf.
Scarlet Emperor Improved. A heavy cropper.
Best of All. Bears fleshy pods in immense clusters.
Streamline. Produces particularly long pods.

HARICOT BEANS

This is an excellent crop to grow under cloches, for there is no difficulty in ripening the pods properly. Sow the seeds in

a similar manner to French beans. Do not pick the pods until
the autumn, when the plants should be pulled up and left to
dry for a few days (if wet, it is necessary to keep them under
cover). The thrashing can be done by putting the plants into
sacks and beating these with sticks.

The beans are stored dry and used throughout the winter.

Varieties
Comtesse de Chambord. The heaviest-cropping white.
Dutch Brown. The best of the brown beans.

PEAS

Pea-guards must be used with outdoor sowings of peas, as
birds are very troublesome. Under continuous cloches, of
course, no pea-guards are necessary. Further, the plants are
protected from being beaten down by wind or rain, and so with
the dwarf varieties no staking is required. Peas can be grown
under cloches the whole time until they are harvested if the
dwarf varieties are chosen for the purpose and the taller cloches
are available.

Soils and Manures. Peas will grow on almost any soil.
They dislike acidity, however, and so liming is a necessity.

Farmyard manure or composted vegetable refuse should be
dug in 7 or 8 inches deep at the rate of one good barrowload to
10 square yards. In addition, a good organic fertiliser should
be forked into the top 3 or 4 inches at 4 or 5 ounces to the
square yard. Also wood ashes, if available, may be applied
at 5 or 6 ounces to the square yard.

Sowing the Seed. Put the cloches in position a week or
10 days before sowing. Draw out drills 2 inches deep and 4
inches wide, and space the seeds out 2 inches apart, zigzag or
staggered. Cover with soil, firm and cover with any tent
cloches, making sure to close the ends with sheets of glass.
Make this first sowing in November or January. As the plants
grow, replace the tent cloches with barn cloches, and finally
with the taller barns, if available. From January sowings the
pods are ready to pick from mid-May onwards.

To prevent mice from getting the seeds put down back-breaking traps baited with marrow seeds. These go easily under the cloches.

Further sowings may be made once a fortnight, if necessary, until the beginning of July. The earliest maturing varieties should be sown at this late season, so as to get good pickings in the month of September and early October. Such sowings usually follow early potatoes or early cauliflowers. Make sure that the soil is damp before sowing the seed, and give it a good flooding beforehand if necessary.

The distance from one row to another depends, of course, on the variety sown. Roughly speaking, give the variety half its height on either side of it. Thus a 3-foot variety needs an 18-inch space on either side and the next row another 18 inches on either side, making in fact 3 feet in all.

General Notes. It is possible, where peas are being grown throughout under the largest cloches, to have a catch-crop of cabbage lettuce or radish on either side of the row.

Good waterings may be given from time to time as advised for French beans.

Harvesting. Pick regularly—making sure not to miss any pods—directly they are ready ; otherwise cropping is impeded.

Varieties

DWARF :

English Wonder. Dwarf, dark, stump-podded. 1 foot.
Kelvedon Wonder. Dark green podded. 1½ feet.
Laxtonian. Good cropper. 1½ feet.
Little Marvel. Stump-podded, very prolific, pods usually in pairs. 1½ feet.
Laxton's Superb. Excellent cropper, fine flavour. 2½ feet.

VERY EARLY :

Meteor. Very heavy cropper. 1 foot. The best cloche variety.

EARLY :

The Clucas. Fine pods. 3 feet.
Blue Bird. Stump-podded. 3 feet.
Foremost. Large podded, good cropper. 3 feet.

MAINCROP :

Onward. Highly recommended. 2½ feet.

SUGAR PEAS

Sugar peas should be grown in exactly the same way as peas. The pods, however, should be pulled when young to be cooked whole, without cutting.   They can either be served hot or can be allowed to get cold and shredded up in salads.

Variety
Paramount.   Heavy cropper.

CHAPTER VIII

THE CABBAGE FAMILY

CONTINUOUS cloches are particularly useful for raising healthy young plants early in the year. Brussels sprouts, for instance, can be produced in a hardy condition from January sowings. Early summer cabbages, such as Primo, can also be got in earlier as the result of cloche covering. The glass tents are most useful for covering spring cabbages early in the year, especially in the north, and in this way they are produced earlier and none will be lost.

BROCCOLI

It is possible with the taller cloches to protect broccoli in the winter, especially if the plants are bent over towards the north. This can be done by taking out a spadeful of soil on the north side of the plant, heeling the plant over, and then putting the soil on the back of the plant. This, however, is rather an uneconomical way of using cloches, and would probably not be followed except in special circumstances in the north.

With broccoli it is possible to produce beautiful white curds from the Michaelmas Day of one year to the middle of June the following year.

Soils and Manures. Broccoli prefers firm soil, and so should follow a crop that has been well manured. Light, sandy soils may have dung or well-rotted vegetable refuse dug in at the rate of one barrowload per 10 square yards. This should be buried 8 inches down. Firming, however, must be done afterwards.

Rake into the top 2 or 3 inches fish manure at 3 to 4 ounces to the square yard and sulphate of potash at $\frac{1}{2}$ ounce to the square yard. When these are unobtainable use wood ashes at 3 ounces per square yard.

Sowing the Seed. Sow seed under cloches early in March, in drills ½ inch deep ; lantern cloches suit seedlings quite well. There is no need to protect the seedlings with black cotton, as must be done when they are sown outside. Seed-rows may be as close as 9 inches apart. Whiten the seeds and space them out 1 inch apart, for under cloches every seed grows.

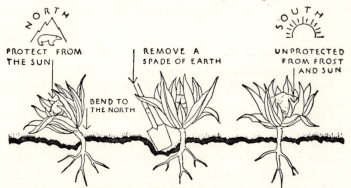

Protect Broccoli in winter by heeling plants over to the North.

It is really only the earliest sowings that need covering with cloches. The later sowings can be sown in the open.

N.B.—This has proved a good use for small tent cloches. Quicker germination is desirable, and seeds are protected from birds and cats.

Planting. Plant after such crops as French beans, early potatoes, early carrots or early peas. Arrange them 2 feet square. Should the weather be dry, put plenty of water in the holes at planting time. Firm well.

General Notes. Hoe regularly. Watch for cabbage-root maggot. Give mercuric chloride treatment or naphthalene if necessary.

Harvesting. Cut directly the curds are ready. If too many turn in at a time, pull them up and hang them by their heels in a shed.

Varieties (*For Autumn*)

Extra Early Roscoff.   Perhaps the most delicious.
Walcheren.   More suitable for the north.

N.B.—There are other varieties—such as New Year for late December, Early Feltham for mid-January, Snow's Winter White for April, Late Feltham for May, and Clucas' June for June—but these can normally be sown out of doors, though the cloche protection will prevent damage from birds.

BROCCOLI, SPROUTING

Sprouting broccoli is a very hardy vegetable, whose elongated flower-heads are delicious to eat. By growing several varieties it is possible to cut from late September to the beginning of April.

Soils and Manures.   As advised for broccoli.

Sowing the Seed.   Sow the seed in April as advised for broccoli.

Planting.   Plant out 2 feet square when ready, on any land available.

Harvesting.   Cut the flower-shoots found growing in the axils of the leaves to within two-thirds of their length, and as a result more shoots will be thrown out on the same stem.   Do not cut the main heads till all the sprouting tips have been consumed.

Varieties

Calabresse.   Usually used in September.   Need $2\frac{1}{2}$ feet by $2\frac{1}{2}$ feet.
Christmas Early Purple.   Cuts just before Christmas and continues many weeks.
Early Purple Sprouting.   Cuts in February and March.
Late Purple Sprouting.   Excellent in April.

BRUSSELS SPROUTS

Sowing the Seed.   Brussels sprouts seeds should be sown as advised for broccoli, at the end of January.   It is a good plan first to whiten the seeds with lime to ensure thin sowing.   Thin out when 2 inches high to 3 inches apart under further cloches.

Plant the young plants in the open ground at the end of April or early May, 3 feet by 3 feet.   It should be possible as a result to harvest the first sprouts late in August.

Pests and Diseases. Look out for the blue bug or blue aphis and spray with liquid derris or nicotine immediately this is seen. (See page 147.)

General Notes. The sprouts should be picked from the bottom of the plant first.

Covering. Tent cloches are quite suitable for sprouts and are usually in use during the months of January, February and March.

Varieties

Cambridge Early No. 1. ⎫ Two excellent Cambridge
Cambridge Late No. 5.   ⎬ University kinds.
Rouslench. A popular "Evesham" type.

CABBAGES

Cloches are useful mainly for spring cabbages, and to produce very early summer cabbages. They need not be used for winter cabbages or savoys.

Soils and Manures. For summer cabbages dig in old farmyard manure or properly composted vegetable refuse at the rate of one barrowload to 10 square yards. In addition, fork in lightly a complete organic fertiliser at 3 to 4 ounces per square yard. For spring cabbages do not dig in farmyard manure, but rely on the organic matter left behind by the previous crop—often potatoes. In spring, however—say February—give blood or soot along the rows at 3 ounces to the yard run.

Lime is always necessary. It should be applied on the surface of the ground before the plants are put out, at say 5 to 7 ounces of hydrated lime per square yard.

General Notes. (a) Early Summer Cabbages. Sow the seed in January or February under tent cloches. Prepare a fine seed-bed. Drills should be $\frac{1}{2}$ inch deep and the seed sown as close as 9 inches apart. Keep the plants under cloches until they are well established. Put them out in the open with 18 inches between the rows and 18 inches between the plants. Hearts usually turn in for use in May.

(b) Spring Cabbages. Normally, spring cabbage seed is

sown in July and transplanted in September or October. Under cloches seed-sowing may be delayed until September and the plants either over-wintered in cloches or put out in the open in early November, spaced out 18 inches by 12 inches.

These cloche-measures need only be undertaken when normal July sowings were forgotten or were not possible. Cloches may be put over the plants in January to give the necessary protection and so get spring cabbages much earlier. It is possible in this way to have a supply of good hearts in March.

Varieties

SPRING :

Clucas' First Early 218. Probably the earliest variety of cabbage known.

Durham Early. Follows above. Delicious hearts.

SUMMER :

Primo. A lovely round " cannon ball ".

Velocity. Small, delicious hearts.

Greyhound. Good flavour, early maturing.

CAULIFLOWERS

Cloches are useful with cauliflowers, for they enable the seeds to be sown much earlier and so curds are fit to cut early in the summer.

Soils and Manures. As advised for cabbages. Firm soil if necessary, as for broccoli.

Sowing the Seed. The first sowing should be made late in August or early in September, under cloches. Sow thinly, and winter the plants under the cloches, putting them out in the open early in April in a sheltered part of the garden. It is sometimes necessary to give extra protection to these plants by covering cloches with sacking during very frosty periods.

The next sowing should be made in January and February. When the plants come through they should be pricked out 4 inches apart under further cloches, which should be put into position over the ground a fortnight beforehand to warm the soil. The plants that result should be put out early in April.

The third sowing should be made under cloches late in March, drills ½ inch deep. Sow the seed thinly—spaced, say,

Roses on St. George's Day under T's.

Lettuce with Parsley " next door ".

How wonderfully well cloches protect against snow and frost.

1. Marrows. 2. Early Beetroot. 3. Radishes—all appreciate these miniature greenhouses.

to 1 inch apart. Thin out and transplant to 3 inches apart, finally planting in the open when land is available.

With all these sowings it is necessary to keep down the club-root disease and take precautions against the cabbage-root maggot when planting out (see page 149).

Planting. Autumn sowings are often planted 1 foot square in March in a sheltered position. It is possible to cover with barn cloches if it is desired that the cauliflowers should turn in extra early.

From the later sowings the plants should be put out $2\frac{1}{2}$ feet apart and 2 feet apart in the rows. Aim always at transplanting early, before the plants get too big.

It is always possible to obtain succession by planting out further batches without continuous cloche protection, or to remove the cloches after a week or two of covering.

General Notes. When the plants start to curd out of doors, bend one or two of the inner leaves over the " flower " to prevent it turning yellow.

Varieties

AUTUMN SOWING :
   Salvo. An early, well-protected type.
   All-the-Year-Round. A compact grower.

JANUARY AND FEBRUARY SOWINGS :
   Snowball. A later All-the-Year-Round.
   Earliest Erfurt. Lovely white curds.
   Forerunner. Does not seed easily.

There are later varieties of cauliflower, such as Majestic, Early Giant, Autumn Mammoth and Improved Autumn Giant, which can be sown in the open, in April or early May, and need not be covered by cloches.
   N.B.—Most Important. Never transplant cauliflowers too deeply, or they go blind.

COLEWORTS

Colewort is a hardy type of cabbage which need not be grown under continuous cloches. It is, however, dwarf and quick to mature, and so gives good results under barn cloches if available. It should only be grown under cloches when a quick return of small-hearted greens is desired.

Sowing the Seed. Sow the seed shallowly, as for cabbage,

c

at any time from April to the end of July. Try to arrange rows 1 foot apart, and sow the seeds in threes, 6 inches apart in the rows. If all three seeds grow per station, thin down to one. Grow under continuous cloches all the time ; the barn type will be necessary.

Variety

Rosette.   Best for under cloches.

KALES AND SAVOYS

Plants may be raised under continuous cloches if necessary, but it is seldom done. Where early kales are desired under cloches, the seed may be put in late in February or early in March.

Savoys are really a type of hardy winter cabbage. The seed should be sown in early March, and the hearts should be ready to cut in September.

In Scotland, cloches have proved excellent for protecting winter savoys and other greens, too.

CHAPTER IX

OTHER VEGETABLES

ONIONS

IT took the war of 1939 to make the country discover how dependent it was on the onion crop. There is no doubt that to get the heaviest crops and largest bulbs it is necessary to sow the seed under glass and to transplant the seedlings later. Cloches are ideal for this purpose, for under them the hardiest little plants are produced, and, as a result, attacks by the onion fly are few and far between. Actually the English onion is more valuable than the Spanish onion from the point of view of food.

Soils and Manures. On the whole, onions do best on a deeply cultivated, rich, sandy loam. They will do well, however, on a much heavier soil, providing this is opened up by the addition of sand, burnt soil or other finely divided gritty matter.

The soil should be dug over a spade's depth sometime before seed-sowing, to allow it to settle down. Farmyard manure or composted vegetable refuse should be buried at least 6 inches deep, at the rate of one good barrowload per 12 square yards, and in addition the following artificials may be forked into the top 3 or 4 inches : steamed bone flour at 4 ounces to the square yard, wood ashes at $\frac{1}{2}$ pound to the square yard, soot at $\frac{1}{4}$ pound to the square yard and, if available, dried powdered poultry manure at 3 ounces to the square yard. Instead of all these, an organic proprietary fertiliser containing at least 7 per cent. potash, 7 per cent. phosphates and 4 per cent. nitrogen may be used.

It is most important to firm the soil before sowing the seed. This may be done either by treading or rolling, but never when the soil is sticky.

All these preparations refer to the land where the onions are to be planted out.

Sowing the Seed. There are two main periods for seed-sowing : (a) in the autumn and (b) in the spring. In the case of the autumn sowings there are two sub-divisions : (i) for salads and (ii) for early summer bulbs. Different varieties have to be grown in each case.

(a) Autumn Sowing. In the case of salad onions, no special preparation of the ground need be carried out as advised above.

It is only necessary to choose soil that was well manured for a previous crop, such as potatoes. The seed should be sown in the latter part of July or the beginning of August. On the whole, the farther north the earlier the sowing. The rows should be 9 inches apart and the drills ½ inch deep. Cover with continuous cloches as soon as these are available from other crops—say early in October. The onions, as a result, are pulled fresh for salad purposes in the spring.

For the early summer " bulbing " onions the same rules hold good, except that the rows should be 1 foot apart. The plants that result, however, are thinned in the spring, the thinnings being transplanted 12 inches between the rows and 6 inches between the plants. Continuous cloches may be put over these rows if particularly early crops are desired. Otherwise the cloches may be released for other crops.

(b) Spring Sowing. Even here it is possible to have two sub-divisions, for those who are going to plant out so as to get the heaviest bulbs should sow in shallow drills in January in rows 4 to 6 inches apart under any cloches. The sowing should be done very thinly. It is even worth while spacing the seeds out to an inch apart, having whitened them with lime first of all, so that they can easily be seen.

N.B.—Four rows 5 inches apart under a barn cloche and, say, two rows 6 inches apart under a tent.

The plants are then grown on under the cloches until April —say the second or third week—when they may be planted into the specially prepared beds as advised, in rows 1 foot apart and 9 inches between the plants.

For those who do not wish to transplant, the seed should be

sown in February or March in rows 1 foot apart, with the drills ½ inch deep. The cloches should be put into position a fort-night before, to make sure that the soil is warm. The seed should be sown thinly. Some prefer to sow three seeds at 6-inch intervals along the rows and to thin the seedlings down to one if the three grow. The cloches should then be left in position until the leaves start to touch the glass, when they may be removed, to be replaced by taller cloches or because the cloches are needed for other crops.

General Notes. Onions should never be transplanted deeply, for if they are they tend to grow like leeks. Any hoeing that is done should be away from the plants rather than up to them.

Care should be taken when transplanting in the open to prevent damage by the onion fly, and whizzed or flaked naphthalene should be used as a preventative.

Harvesting. The bulbs should ripen naturally in Septem-ber, but to help them the tops are usually bent over at the neck. It is then that the continuous cloches, if available, may be put over, for these help considerably in the ripening-off process. A few weeks later it should be possible to pull the onions up and lay them on their sides, still under cloches, when the bottoms will dry off properly.

Varieties

AUTUMN SOWING :
  SALAD :
    White Lisbon. The favourite variety for pulling green.
    New Queen. To be grown where White Lisbon has proved subject to disease.

  SUMMER BULBING :
    Giant Rocca. A long-keeping onion of good size.
    Unwin's Reliance. One of the heaviest-cropping varieties there is.

SPRING SOWING :
  JANUARY FOR PLANTING OUT :
    The Premier. A huge onion of exhibition type.
    Selected Ailsa Craig. Produces very large, heavy bulbs.

  FEBRUARY-MARCH SOWINGS *in situ* :
    Bedfordshire Champion. Good bulbs of mild flavour.
    Rousham Park Hero. An excellent keeper, popular in the north.

CELERY

Celery growing may be divided into two main groups : (a) the celery that is grown in trenches and (b) the celery that is grown on the top of the ground and almost blanches itself.

To get the best results it is always necessary to sow celery seed under glass. Most people raise plants by sowing in a greenhouse in January or February. The sowing is done in boxes, the seedlings being transplanted into further boxes, then into frames and finally into their permanent position.

By raising celery plants under continuous cloches, much time and labour are saved, and hardier and better plants result. Cloches are *not* used throughout the growth of the plants, though this is possible with self-bleaching celery if the taller barn cloches are available.

Celery in Trenches

Sowing the Seed. Purchase seed that is guaranteed free from the spores of the phoma root rot and septoria blight. Such seed is now available.

Sow the seed in the shallowest of drills, 4 to 6 inches apart, sprinkling it so that it falls about $\frac{1}{8}$ inch apart. Whiten the seeds first with lime, to make them more visible in the soil. Rake the soil over lightly and cover with cloches, being sure to seal up the ends of the row with sheets of glass.

N.B.—Rows should be 5 inches apart under the cloches.

The sowing should be done in mid-February or early March on soil that has been enriched with horticultural peat lightly raked in at, say, half a bucketful to the square yard.

Thinning and Transplanting. Thin the seedlings out to 6 inches apart when they have developed three or four leaves, and transplant the thinnings to 4 inches square under further cloches. Again see that there is plenty of organic matter in the top 6 inches of soil by forking in horticultural peat or similar material at half a bucketful to the square yard. As a result the plants will be properly developed and of a good size by the beginning of June, when they should be transferred to their permanent quarters in trenches 9 inches apart.

Frost Protection. Barn cloches can be used once more to cover the rows early in the winter, when frost and rain may threaten to spoil the crop. Cloche-covered rows of celery keep going until the middle of March.

Varieties

White Perfection. Produces solid, firm sticks. Crisp, of good flavour.
Clayworth Prize Pink. Excellent quality. Keeps well.
Red Standard. Solid sticks of good size.
Covent Garden Red. Excellent flavour.

Self-Bleaching Celery

Crops of self-bleaching celery keep going until the middle of November. This is an interesting crop for the cloche user, for it saves him digging trenches, and, further, he has celery to use much earlier in the year.

Sowing the Seed. As for ordinary celery.

Thinning and Transplanting. As for ordinary celery.

Planting Out. The soil used for planting out should be enriched with plenty of well-rotted farmyard manure or composted straw or refuse. In addition, a good fish manure, a meat and bone meal or a good organic fertiliser should be lightly forked in at 5 to 6 ounces per square yard.

The plants should be set out in rows either 9 inches or 1 foot apart, depending on the cloches to be used, and 1 foot apart in the rows in either case. The ground should be well soaked with water before planting, and during the season it will be necessary to give thorough soakings with water once a week or so when the weather is dry. Little drills may be drawn out on either side of the rows of continuous cloches to act as water " conduits ".

Blanching. In order to help self-bleaching celery to blanch properly, it is a good plan to use barn cloches to cover, say, a row at a time. The inside of the cloches should be whitewashed, and the sheet at the end of each row used to close up the ends whitewashed too, or squares of asbestos can be used instead. Such cloches act as blanchers, being used in September. It usually takes about 14 days for the plants to become fully white.

Harvesting. This can be done directly the celery is sufficiently blanched.

Varieties

Doré. The best pure white dwarf. Of good flavour.
Golden Marvel Blanching. Very solid, blanches easily.

LEEKS

As the severest of winters cannot harm leeks, the use of cloches is concerned entirely with the raising of the plants. They are a valuable vegetable, for they can be used in the winter when other vegetables are scarce, and may be dug up as and when required.

Sowing the Seed. This should be done in January, February or early March, as advised for onions. The earlier the sowing, naturally the earlier the crop, and for the sake of continuity it is a good plan to make three small sowings under continuous cloches, say on the 5th January, February and March.

Thin and shallow sowing is important, as in the case of onions, and plenty of finely divided organic matter, such as de-acidified peat, should be forked into the top 3 or 4 inches, so that a good root system may be formed early in the plant's life.

Transplanting. The tent cloches may be left in position over the leeks until the leaves reach the top. Then they may be transplanted into their permanent quarters, with about 1 foot between the rows and 8 inches apart in the rows.

To get the best plants it is advisable to thin out the seedlings in their early stages and transplant under further cloches, again as advised for onions.

Varieties

Emperor. A medium variety. Very suitable for the north.
The Lyon. Good thick white stems. Delicious flavour.
Walton Mammoth. An early variety. Mild, agreeable flavour.
Giant Musselburgh. Long, thick, white stems. Popular in midlands.
Monarch. Produces an enormous stem. One of the best flavoured.

SHALLOTS

Shallots are one of the easiest vegetables to grow, and they are quite hardy. Some people, however, like to cover them with continuous cloches after planting, for then they are never disturbed by birds, and, because of the extra warmth given by the cloches, they start away earlier, giving heavier yields as a result.

The cloches should only be left in position for a month or 6 weeks.

Planting should be done so that the rows are about 1 foot apart and the bulbs spaced out 4 inches apart in the rows. Quite a good place to plant shallots is along the tops of celery trenches, or to form an edging to a path.

Ripening. It is possible to help shallots to ripen properly if cloches are put over the top when the leaves start to turn yellow. You must not close the ends in this case, as you want the air to circulate.

Varieties

The Russian Shallot, sometimes called the **Dutch** or **Jersey Shallot.** Produces a large, round bulb.

The True (red or yellow) **Shallot.** Does not produce as large a bulb as the above variety, but gives a nice firm bulb of the right size for pickling. Keeps well.

SPINACH

There are two types of spinach : the winter spinach, which has prickly seeds, and the summer spinach, which has round seeds. The winter spinach in the normal way is sown to live through the autumn, and the summer spinach in the spring. Under cloches, however, it is a good plan to sow the prickly-seeded types all the year round.

It is possible, under cloches, to have spinach in use 6 weeks before normal sowings are possible outside.

Soils and Manures. Spinach will grow on almost any soil. When preparing the ground, old farmyard manure or compost (see page 20) should be dug in, 8 inches down, at the rate of one good barrowload to 10 square yards. In addition, meat and bone meal, hoof and horn meal, a good fish manure or any of the well-known organic proprietary

C*

fertilisers should be forked in at 4 to 5 ounces to the square yard.

Sowing the Seed. Under cloches this may be done at almost any time of the year. Winter sowings are particularly successful. It is a good plan to make a sowing once a month from October until February, for it is usually during the winter and very early spring that greens are scarce.

Aim at having the drills 1 foot apart and 1 inch deep. Sow the seed very thinly and, directly the seedlings are large enough to be handled, thin to 6 inches apart, transplanting the thinnings under further cloches if necessary.

In the case of very wet soil it is advisable to sow the seed on raised beds. These may be, say, 5 feet wide and 3 inches above the level of the surrounding soil. It is quite possible to have the rows as close as 8 inches apart if this makes it convenient to fit them under the size of cloches available.

General Notes. Those who are going to use continuous cloches for spinach in the summer will find that they have to give regular floodings if they are to prevent the spinach from going to seed. Cloches, however, are better used for other crops during hot weather.

Winter spinach should not be picked too hard, the largest leaves being taken each time. In the case of summer spinach under cloches it is better to pull up the whole plant when ready, and use it.

Varieties

New Giant-leaved. Prickly-seeded, long-standing, large leaved.
New Prickly. Hardy, crops heavily.
Monstrous Viroflay. Round-seeded, really a summer variety.

SPINACH BEET

This is a perpetual spinach which may be started under cloches. The seed should be sown late in March, though it is possible to make another sowing out of doors in August.

The rows should be 15 inches apart and the plants thinned out to this distance.

A month or 6 weeks after seed-sowing it should be possible to remove the cloches and use them for other crops.

SEAKALE SPINACH

The stems are wide and ivory-white, and are used as seakale, while the leaves at the top are used as spinach. It is a crop of biennial type, and goes on producing both leaves and stems for months at a time.

Soils and Manures. As for beetroot (see page 47).

Sowing the Seed. The rows should be 18 inches apart and the plants should be thinned to 15 inches apart in the rows.

General Notes. Cloches are used if necessary to start this crop off well, and the tomato " T " cloches prove useful in the winter for covering the rows to keep out the damp and frost. The plants thus go on cropping through the cold, wet periods.

NEW ZEALAND SPINACH

New Zealand spinach is an invaluable summer vegetable which should be more widely grown. It goes on cropping until well on in October and never seems affected by the hottest weather. Normally, plants have to be raised under glass and put out late in May, for the New Zealand spinach is susceptible to frost.

Sowing the Seed. It is possible under continuous cloches to sow the seed in April where the plants are to grow. The drills should be 1 inch deep, and the seed should be spaced out 4 inches apart.

Transplanting. Directly the spinach is large enough to handle it should be transplanted into rows 3 feet apart, leaving 2 feet between the plants. Cloche covering will again be necessary, and it is sometimes convenient to cover each plant individually with a four-sided cloche for this purpose. New Zealand spinach plants transplant better if the original soil in which they are sown had plenty of finely divided organic matter, such as horticultural peat, incorporated into the top 3 or 4 inches.

Another method is to sink 3-inch pots up to their rims in the ground, as close to one another as possible, and having filled them with John Innes compost (see page 91) to sow one seed in each. The plants can then be left in the pots for 6 weeks or more, when they can be transplanted into the open.

General Notes. When the plants creep along the ground and spread out too wide for the cloches, these should be removed and used for other crops. Keep the ground hoed between the plants as long as possible, and when the weather is dry give soakings with water, if available.

VEGETABLE MARROWS

Soils and Manures. Marrows are commonly grown on heaps, either those made up specially for the purpose or on the ordinary rubbish heap. Actually they do well in any soil, providing this is heavily manured. With clay soils and in wet years they prefer growing on a slight mound, for, as a result, their roots will be drier, but with light soils and in dry years they do best on the flat.

As much organic material as possible should be dug into the soil where the marrows are to grow.   It is a good plan to make furrows 9 inches deep and to half fill these with well-decayed manure or compost. This should then be trodden down and the soil replaced, thus forming a ridge over the manure. A certain amount of bottom heat is generated, and the plants get away quickly in consequence. In addition to the organic manure used, a complete organic fertiliser should be forked into the top 2 or 3 inches at 3 or 4 ounces to the square yard.

Sowing the Seed. The seeds may either be sown under lantern cloches where the plants are to grow, or in pots sunk into the ground to rim level, side by side under a row of continuous cloches. The pots should be filled with a mixture consisting of 2 parts soil, 1 part horticultural peat and 1 part coarse silver sand, adding to each 3-gallon bucketful of this mixture 1½ ounces of superphosphate and 1 ounce of ground limestone or chalk.

One seed should be sown ½ inch deep in the centre of each pot, and having plunged the pots into the centre of the rows close together up to their rims, they should be covered with large tent or low barn cloches, closing the ends with sheets of glass.

The seeds should be sown about the second week of April, and should there be danger of frost at night, the cloches should be covered with old sacks or hessian. It will be necessary to water the pots from time to time, but the plants can grow on in their pots under the cloches until the characteristic leaves have developed, the planting out being done after all fear of frost is passed—say about the 20th May.

It is possible, of course, to sow the seed *in situ*, *i.e.*, where the plants are to grow—at the end of March in warm districts and in mid-April in the colder parts. Bush varieties sown 3 feet apart are the best. Stations are prepared where the seeds are sown as advised on page 76 for the reception of the plants. The centre part where the seed is to be sown should be slightly higher than the rest of the ground.

Transplanting. If it is desired to go on growing the marrows under large barn cloches, the plants should be put out in rows, 3 feet apart, giving 3 feet between the plants. Each plant will have its own large barn cloche covering it, the ends being closed with sheets of glass. The cloche is then left in position until the plant fills it completely, the end-pieces of glass being removed some time in June.

When growing trailing marrows to climb up fences, pergolas or wire netting, the plants should be 4 feet apart, and should be put in 1 foot away from the fence or post. A special hole may be prepared for each one, a spade's depth and a spade's width, burying a forkful of compost at the bottom of each as advised previously under the ridge system. The plants are then put into position and covered with large lantern-type cloches, these being removed when the trailers start to grow.

Varieties

On the flat the bush-type marrows should be grown. Two good varieties are **Bush-shaped Green** and **Bush-shaped White.**

For climbing, **Long Green** is to be recommended, and so is the white trailing type known as **Clucas' Roller.**

    Rotherside Orange. Bears flattened, globe-shaped fruits of a beautiful golden colour and of a delicate flavour.

    Stonor's Universal. Very suitable for cloche work.

    White Custard. Most attractive shape with fluted edges.

POTATOES

Continuous cloches can be used for raising particularly early potatoes.

Soils and Manures. The ideal soil is a deep, well-drained loam, neither too heavy nor too light. The land should be prepared by deep working, the organic manure used being placed into the drills at planting time. It is foolish to apply artificials for very early potatoes, for the tubers are out of the ground before they can make use of this extra plant food.

The Tubers. Certified Scotch or Irish seed should be used, about the size of a hen's egg. This should be obtained in December or early January, and the tubers should be placed in trays or shallow boxes in an airy, frost-proof shed with plenty of light. A greenhouse is excellent for this purpose.

Shoots, sprouts or sprits should then develop, and by the second week of February these should be $\frac{1}{2}$ to 1 inch long. Only two shoots should be allowed on each potato at planting time.

Planting. Planting should be carried out at the end of the second week of February. The ground should be levelled a week beforehand, and large tent or barn cloches should be put in continuous rows in position where the potatoes are to be planted.

At the end of the week the cloches should be removed and a drill 4 inches deep drawn out. Into this may be placed a thick layer of well-rotted farmyard manure or good compost, and on top the tubers should be planted, 1 foot apart. Cover the potatoes with soil, drawing a ridge 2 inches high right down the row. Put the continuous cloches back into position and close the ends with sheets of glass, kept in position by a strong wire or a narrow post.

General Notes. Large tent cloches may be used to start with, but as the potatoes grow these should be removed and the taller barn cloches substituted. During the change over, which is usually done when the plants are 6 or 7 inches high, earthing-up may take place. The soil should be drawn up to the plants 3 or 4 inches.

Harvesting. The potatoes may be dug about the middle

of May, starting at one end of the row and gradually working to the other end. The sheet of glass at the end of the row should be replaced each time.

Intercrops. Radishes or lettuces may be grown on either side of the rows as an intercrop, providing the latter are cut before they are fully hearted.

CHAPTER X

SALADS

CONTINUOUS cloches are ideal for all salad crops, for underneath them the plants grow naturally, and yet receive no check. The extra sunshine the cloches seem to gather together ensures that quick growth which is so necessary to the succulent tastiness much desired in these crops.

ENDIVE

This is a salad which is much used on the Continent and is becoming increasingly popular in England.

Soils and Manures. Almost any soil will grow endive well, providing it is rich in organic matter. Grow this crop, therefore, on land that has been previously well treated with dung or organic matter, and if this is impossible, dig in well-rotted farmyard manure or composted vegetable refuse, burying it 7 or 8 inches down. In addition, fork into the top 3 or 4 inches fish manure, meat and bone meal, hoof and horn meal or any other good complete organic fertiliser. Use either of these at 4 or 5 ounces to the square yard.

Sowing the Seed. Rake the soil down level and work into fine particles. A week or ten days before the seeds are to be sown, place the cloches in position to warm the soil. Draw out drills about ¾ inch deep and 1 foot apart. Sow the seeds in threes, 12 inches apart along the drills, thinning the seedlings down to one if all three grow. Such seedlings may be transplanted if necessary, but the best hearts are assured if the seeds are sown where the plants are to grow.

After sowing, rake down level again and cover with continuous cloches, closing up the ends of the rows with a sheet of glass.

For a continuous supply, four main sowings are possible :

(i) mid-June, (ii) mid-July, (iii) mid-August and (iv) mid-September.

Blanching. When the plants are fully grown they should be blanched before being used. This is best done by removing the cloches and coating the insides thickly with whitewash before putting them back into position again. The sheet of glass at the ends of each row should be treated in a similar manner.

Where it is not desired to whitewash the panes of glass, it is possible to remove them and to put in similar sized squares of asbestos sheets. These are excellent for blanching the endive and once this operation has been concluded the glass can be put back again. It takes a long time to wash off the whitewash and so many gardeners prefer the asbestos, and some have actually got a special reserve of asbestos cloches for use during the winter months.

General Notes. Should the weather be dry, draw out drills on either side of the cloche rows, filling these up with water from time to time. Do not water during the week before blanching.

Varieties

Moss-curled. Leaves crinkly and crisp.
Green Batavian. Leaves more like a lettuce. The most popular in Great Britain.

CORN SALAD

Corn salad is sometimes known as Lamb's lettuce—a salad crop which is much neglected, and which comes in very useful from Christmas onwards.

Soils and Manures. The ground should be prepared as advised for endive.

Sowing the Seed. The seed should be sown at three periods—mid-June, mid-July and mid-September, thus continuity throughout the winter is assured.

The rows should be 8 inches apart, the drills $\frac{1}{2}$ inch deep, and the seedlings thinned to 8 inches apart in the drills.

Although seed-sowing may be carried out in the open, the

highest germination results when the rows are covered with continuous cloches.

General Notes.   The leaves of the corn salad resemble the forget-me-not, and may either be gathered one at a time or whole plants may be pulled up and used at once.   The cloche-covering is best done from late October onwards, and the great advantage is that the plants are kept clean and little washing has to be done before they are used in salads.

Varieties

Round-leaved.   Dark, very delicious.
Regence.   Has more pointed leaves.

LETTUCE

Lettuces are undoubtedly one of the best crops for growing under continuous cloches.   They enable the gardener to produce plants with beautiful hearts almost all the year round. Plants grown under cloches turn in three weeks or a month sooner than similar sowings made in the open.   Naturally, to get these results it is necessary to choose a sunny place for the early spring and autumn crops, so that the plants can obtain the maximum sunshine for that time of the year.

Soils and Manures.   You cannot expect to produce first-class lettuces unless your soil is well cultivated and generously manured.   The land should, therefore, be bastard-trenched, old farmyard manure or composted vegetable refuse being buried a spade's depth, at the rate of one good bucketful to the square yard.   In addition, a good horticultural peat should be worked into the top 2 or 3 inches at the rate of half a 2-gallon bucketful to the square yard.   If the soil is dry, this peat should be damped first of all.   At the same time, incorporate a good organic fertiliser, such as fish manure or meat and bone meal, at the rate of a good handful to the square yard.

Rake the surface level, remove all the large stones and bits of debris, and put the cloches into position lined up in a continuous row, sealing the ends of the rows with sheets of glass held in position by bamboos or metal rods thrust into the soil and wired to the nearest cloche handle.   Put the cloches into position to warm up the soil a week or more before sowing or transplanting.

Sowing the Seed. It is most important with lettuces to sow the right varieties at the right time. Some kinds are best adapted to the spring period, when the days are short. Others only thrive in the long, sunny days of summer. Never sow lettuce seed deeper than about ¼ inch ; it saves a tremendous amount of thinning to sow two or three seeds at stations the right distances apart, rather than to sow in a complete row.

There are six main sowings :

Sowing No. 1. The first sowing should be made early in January or, in the north, about mid-February. The rows should be 7 or 8 inches apart, the outside ones being approximately 4 inches away from the glass sides of the cloches when these are in position. Naturally the number of rows will depend on the width of the cloche. Immediately after sowing draw a small amount of the soil into the drill with an iron rake used upside down—so as to cover the seed. Put the cloches back into position and close the ends of the rows with sheets of glass.

Late in February or early in March, the lettuce seedlings will need thinning. If you have sown in stations, your object will be to thin down to one plant per station, but if you have sown in a continuous row, you must thin out to 2 inches apart, and then, three weeks later, to 4 inches apart. A fortnight after that thin to 8 inches apart. The plants that remain will then develop rapidly, and produce good hearts for use in May.

The seedlings of the first and second thinnings can be transplanted under other cloches, and will provide good hearts later in May or early in June. The little plants from the last thinning should not be transplanted, but used as a salad.

The best varieties for these first sowings are May King, sometimes known as May Queen, Feltham King and Market Favourite.

Sowing No. 2. The second sowing should take place during the third week of March in a similar manner to the first sowing, only at thinning time it is necessary to give the plants 10 or

12 inches apart, for they tend to grow larger.   The thinnings from this sowing do not transplant well, and if they *have* to be moved, choose a dull, damp day and a piece of ground that contains plenty of moisture-holding material.

This crop does not need the protection of cloches after the middle of May.   They may therefore be removed and used for another crop.   Good varieties for this sowing are Market Favourite, Improved Trocadero and Webb's Wonderful.   The latter is known as an Iceberg Lettuce, and produces thicker, crisper, curlier leaves than most varieties.   It is particularly delicious.

Sowing No. 3.   It is most important with this sowing to see that there is plenty of fine organic matter in the soil.   It is even worth while to fork in a bucketful of damp horticultural peat to the square yard, because the lettuces will have to withstand drought conditions in the summer.   Many gardeners water the seed-beds thoroughly two days before sowing, in such a manner that the water goes down 4 inches.

This sowing is made during the middle of May, and can be done without cloches.

The best varieties are Market Favourite, All-the-Year-Round and Continuity.

Sowing No. 4.   This sowing is made in the open, but in such a manner and so spaced as to allow cloches to cover the crops at the end of September.   Gardeners often make two sowings at this period, one on the 10th August and the other on the 20th August.   The lettuces that result are cut in October and November.

Good varieties to be used for this sowing are Unrivalled, Sutton's Imperial and Feltham King.

Sowing No. 5.   This is regarded by most cloche-users as the most important sowing of all.   It should produce beautiful, firm-hearted specimens to cut during the whole of April and early May.   Prepare the ground thoroughly, and place the cloches in position at the beginning of October.   Sow the seed about the 14th October, though in the north it may be advisable to sow a week or two before this.   Sow thinly, and when the two seed leaves have fully developed the seedlings should be thinned to 4 inches apart. Please note the importance of thinning as early as this. These baby seedlings with only two leaves may be transplanted under other cloches in such a manner that the foliage is above the surface soil. During January a further thinning is done to 8 inches apart, and the second thinnings may be transplanted under other cloches to 8 inches apart also.

The best varieties for this sowing are May King (sometimes called May Queen) and Attractie.

Sowing No. 6. In the midlands and the south it is customary to sow seeds under cloches in late October or early November, and then to transplant the seedlings as soon as the seed leaves are fully developed, 3 inches apart each way under further cloches. Here the little plants grow on until March, when they are planted out into the open and produce good heads in May or June.

The best varieties for this purpose are May King and Attractie.

General Notes. Though six main sowing periods have been given, it is possible to sow a pinch of seed regularly every ten days from early March until the end of July.

Cos lettuces may be grown under cloches as a spring crop, and do best planted in the centre of a large cloche row with a row of the cabbage type on either side. They may be sown under cloches in the autumn, and the plants from such sowings are then put out into the open ground in March.

The best Cos varieties are Lobjoit's Green and Paris Green.

RADISHES

Radishes can be grown under continuous cloches as a catch-crop, as an intercrop or as a crop on their own at almost any time of the year. The results are particularly valuable when sowings are made under cloches during the months of January, February, March and early April. Cloche-grown radishes are crisp and hard, and are never fibrous and " hot ".

Soils and Manures. Any soil will do, preferably one on the light side. No special manuring is necessary. It is advisable, however, to see that there is plenty of organic matter, such as horticultural peat, in the top 3 or 4 inches, so the soil may be treated as advised for endive.

Sowing the Seed.   Sow the seed shallowly and very thinly as they need to be ½ inch apart, watering the drills should the weather be dry.   Cover the ground with cloches for at least a week before sowing, and again immediately after sowing, and firm, succulent roots will be produced.

General Notes.   Sowings may be made in shallow drills between the rows of lettuces or on both sides of a single row. They may also be made in the same drill as lettuce, carrot, or onion seed, etc., the radishes being pulled early.

Varieties

Sparkler 50/50.   Half red, half white.
French Breakfast.   Perhaps the most delicious.
Crimson Glow.   Turns in quickly.
Scarlet Globe.   A lovely crimson colour.

MUSTARD AND CRESS

There is no difficulty at all in growing mustard and cress under continuous cloches at almost any time of the year except January and February.   The soil should be well enriched with finely divided organic matter such as peat, as advised for endive.   The seed should be sown on the surface of the ground after it has been got down to a fine tilth or, if preferred, on damp sacking laid on the ground for the purpose.   This ensures that the salad keeps free from grit.   A good soaking with water should then be given if the weather is dry, the cloches being put into position immediately afterwards and the ends of the short rows closed with a sheet of glass.   Cut with scissors.   Do not pull up.   Sow cress three days before mustard.

CUCUMBERS

The growing of cucumbers under cloches can be divided roughly into (a) the production of the ridge varieties, and (b) the production of frame varieties.

The ridge types are started off under cloches, and go on growing in the open afterwards.   The frame cucumbers have to be grown under cloches the whole time.   Other than this, the preparation of the soil is very similar. Frame varieties are normally sown under glass and planted out ; ridge varieties are generally sown *in situ*. Frame varieties go bitter if they are pollinated, and so the male blossoms have to be removed ; with ridge varieties this does not matter.

Soils and Manures. Prepare the ground as advised for melons, see page 117. Cucumbers demand rich conditions as far as organic matter is concerned.

Sowing the Seed. Seed sowing may be done in three ways :

(1) In 3-inch pots (either paper or earthenware) sunk to the rims in the soil outside and covered with a large barn cloche made into a hand-light by closing the ends with a sheet of glass.

(2) Three inches apart and ½ inch deep in a properly pre-pared seed-bed under cloches for transplanting later, or

(3) At permanent stations where the plant is intended to grow. (The best method of all.)

In the last case the seed is sown in the centre of the mound by making a slight depression like a saucer and sowing the seed as soon as the temperature of the ground is 60 degrees F. This will usually be about the middle of April in the south, the end of April in the midlands and the beginning of May in the north. By putting the cloches into position seven to ten days before-hand, the soil will be warmed. The butt of a pencil makes a nicely shaped hole, and it is usual to sow three seeds 1 inch apart under each cloche at each station. If the lantern cloche is used, two seeds may do, and the lantern will be replaced by a larger barn cloche directly the growth of the plants makes it necessary.

Planting Out. Where plants are raised in the greenhouse or under cloches, it is usual to transplant the seedlings to the stations where they are to grow directly they have made their first pair of true leaves. Here they will usually be placed 3 feet apart. Ridge varieties should be kept covered till they fill the cloches. Frame varieties are usually kept permanently covered and trained along a horizontal wire stretched tightly just underneath the head of the cloches.

Stopping and Pollination. There is no need to stop ridge varieties after the first stopping at the seventh leaf, and all that needs to be done to the frame types is to stop them at one leaf beyond the forming cucumber. A lateral will then form, and this, in its turn, is stopped at one leaf beyond the cucumber, and so on. These laterals are usually tied to the wires as the work proceeds. It is possible, however, to allow both types of cucumber to grow at will.

Pinch off the male blooms from the frame varieties to prevent them pollinating the female blossoms, as this makes the cucumbers bitter. The male flowers, however, are needed in the case of ridge varieties, and these should not be removed, because they ensure a better set and yet no bitterness.

Ventilation and Feeding. Ridge varieties will, of course, need no special ventilation, as the cloches will be removed sometime early in June. In the case of frame cucumbers, treat them as for melons, see page 118.

Feed as advised for melons, using Liquinure.

Harvesting. Cut the cucumbers as desired. Never let them become too old. Keep cutting, therefore, when they are of a good size, and the plants will keep cropping. It is possible to get forty good cucumbers from a ridge variety, and about half that number from a good frame type.

Varieties

Hampshire Giant. Best of all ridge types. Large cucumbers; plants crop heavily. Fruits almost spineless.

Stockwood Ridge ⎱ Two good ridge varieties, but neither
Bedford Prize Ridge ⎰ as large as Hampshire Giant.

Conqueror. The best of the frame varieties for continuous cloche work.

Telegraph. Use this variety when it is impossible to get Conqueror.

N.B.—The ridge varieties are easy to grow and should be tried by the beginner.

The frame varieties are more popular and have a better flavour on the whole, and so should be grown after some experience.

CHAPTER XI

TOMATOES

ONE of the great advantages of using cloches for tomato growing is that (a) the plants can be put out much earlier, and (b) they can be protected from the frost in the autumn and so all the fruits that develop can be made to ripen properly. Tomato growing under cloches, indeed, is a system which ensures heavy yields without any fear of frost trouble. It enables the northern gardener to grow tomatoes in the open just as easily as his southern friend. The cloche grower does not meet with the difficulties encountered by the greenhouse grower because the former can rotate his tomatoes and this means that he has them in one part of the garden one year and in another part the next, and thus his soil never becomes tomato " sick ".

Raising the Plants. When raising tomatoes, attention must be paid to hygiene and smokers must be careful to wash their hands in strong disinfectant, for the viruses which infect tobacco plants are never killed during the curing. It has been proved that nicotine-stained fingers transmit various virus diseases, and it is important, therefore, to either (a) refrain from smoking or (b) see that the hands are properly " sterilised " before they handle plants. In addition, of course, the pots and boxes should be quite clean and at the Horticultural Training Centre we dip pots and boxes as a rule in a tank containing a 2 per cent. solution of formaldehyde for 48 hours.

It may be necessary to sterilise the soil used for the John Innes Compost and a simple way of doing this is to fill a bucket with loam and hang it from a cross bar laid over a copper of boiling water. The bucket should be suspended so that the water reaches within an inch of the top and should never bubble inside. If a potato the size of an egg is buried in the centre of the soil 1 inch down then the gardener will know that when the potato is cooked, the earth is correctly sterilised.

If this rule of thumb method does not seem sufficiently scientific, an alternative scheme is to use a copper and fit into this some perforated zinc on a wooden framework, so that this barrier lies about 6 inches above the curved base. Then 2 gallons of water can be put into the bottom of the copper, and on the framework provided a perforated bucket can be stood filled with dry soil. The water should then be made to boil so that the soil in the bucket reaches a temperature of 210 degrees F. in half an hour. A top is, of course, placed on the copper to keep the heat in. Ten minutes after this the soil should be sterilised and ready for use. If a soil thermometer is used it is possible to test the temperature and make certain that the soil is heated for the right period at the right degree, *i.e.*, 210 degrees F.

Sometimes it is impossible to use steam and so chemical sterilisers must be employed. In this case the scheme is to employ either formaldehyde which kills all the diseases or cresylic acid which will kill all the pests. There is no chemical steriliser which will do both at the same time. Water the soil to be sterilised with a 2 per cent. solution, adding 1 gallon of 40 per cent. strength formaldehyde to 49 gallons of water, and cover with formalin-soaked sacks for 48 hours to keep in the volatile gas. The soil should then be spread out as thinly as possible to dry and not used for propagation till all trace of formaldehyde smell has disappeared. If you are going to use cresylic acid you will need a 2½ per cent. solution—this is made by pouring 1 gallon of 99 per cent. strength cresylic acid into 39 gallons of water and stirring well. This should be watered on to the soil in the same way as formaldehyde, the only difference being that the workers must wear protective clothing for damage can be caused by contact with the acid.

Compost Under Cloches. When the tomatoes are sown in pots in the greenhouse the John Innes Compost is used and so the soil under the cloches should be treated in a similar way. Appropriate proportions of horticultural peat and sand should be mixed into the top 6 inches of soil together with the necessary plant foods and lime. Another method is to remove the top 2 or 3 inches of soil and replace it with a carefully prepared compost mixture. It is always worth while taking the utmost trouble in preparing the soil.

Dates of Sowing. These will, of course, conform to the dates that the plants are required for putting out in the garden and the table below gives some guidance :

Cloche-Raised Plants

Variety	Date Sown	Date Transplanted	Date De-cloched	Date First pick
Outdoor	Mar. 27	June 10	June 28	July 28
Open Air	Mar. 31	June 15	June 29	Aug. 24

Sowing the Seeds. It has been made clear above that the soil under the cloches is to be made as similar to the John Innes Compost as possible, the formula for this being 2 parts by bulk of good soil, 1 part of horticultural peat and 1 part of coarse sand. To this compost is added 1½ ounces of superphosphate and ¾ ounce of ground chalk per bushel, and a bushel of soil goes exactly in a box 22 inches long, 10 inches wide and 10 inches deep.

The method, therefore, is to add the horticultural peat, sand, superphosphate and lime, and then to fork this along the strip to be covered by the cloches. In cases where the soil has been used again and again for cloche crops it is worth while sterilising the strip of soil beforehand by watering with a 2 per cent. solution of formaldehyde at the rate of 2 gallons to the yard run, then covering with cloches and putting sacks over these for two days. At the end of 48 hours, remove the cloches and fork the soil up each day for a week so as to disperse all traces of fumes. Incidentally, the superphosphate and lime are usually added at 3 ounces to the yard run, the peat at a bucketful to the yard run and the coarse sand at a similar rate. If the soil is heavy but the land very sandy, naturally the coarse sand dressing may be omitted.

Some gardeners remove the top 2 or 3 inches of soil which is going to be exactly under the cloches and replace this with the

John Innes Compost—this takes longer but one does know that the soil mixture is perfect. In both cases, the seeds should be sown $1\frac{1}{2}$ inches square and $\frac{1}{4}$ inch deep. Shade the cloches by throwing a few sacks here and there after sowing until the seedlings are well developed, and either transplant the seedlings to their permanent positions from where they are growing by getting them up carefully with a trowel, or pot them up into paper pots when they are 3 inches high or into home-made " soil blocks ". Put the potted plants into a trench 3 inches deep cut to the appropriate width and length so that the cloches can be placed over the top to cover the plants.

Watering may have to be done from time to time but it will be found that plants under continuous cloches never dry out as quickly as they do in the greenhouse.

General Notes

(1) Always handle the seedlings with clean hands and never squeeze the stems in any way.

(2) Never transplant during cold, windy weather.

(3) Always use reliable healthy seed.

(4) Be ready to give protection during excessive frost or sunshine during the earlier part of the season.

(5) Tend to under water rather than over water.

(6) Look out for the rogues known as feather-heads or Christmas trees. These plants have a dwarf leafy appearance with more side shoots. They must be destroyed in the early stages.

(7) Don't handle the plants with nicotine stains on the fingers.

Preparation of Soil and Site. Any properly prepared soil will grow tomatoes, although heavy clay will need to be bastard trenched in the autumn as described earlier and can be improved by working in plenty of strawy manure or even chopped straw. Light soils need plenty of well-rotted vegetable matter or dung. Dig this in about a spade's depth and in addition apply horticultural peat—this should be soaked well first. Light soils are likely to be lacking in potash and so wood ashes or sulphate of potash should be applied.

Take out a trench 1 foot deep and 2 feet wide at the end of

the border, removing this soil to the other end where it can be used for filling the last trench.   Be sure to pick out any perennial weed roots which are seen and remove the little shining globular eggs of slugs and other pests.   Apply the hydrated lime afterwards at the rate of 5 to 6 ounces to the square yard when the tomatoes are to be planted on the flat.   When planting in a trench dig the ground over and leave it rough and only dig the organic matter into it when the trench is being prepared, *i.e.*, a fortnight before planting.

Don't forget in either case to use horticultural peat at half a bucketful to the square yard and a complete organic fertiliser like hoof and horn meal to which potash has been added at 4 to 5 ounces to the square yard.   These ingredients are forked into the top 3 inches of soil either in the trench or on the flat, preferably about ten days before planting.

Trenches. Many gardeners have found that trench planting gives excellent results because it gives the cloches the extra height and therefore the plants can stay under them for a longer period.   Dig the trenches out a spade's depth and a spade's width, throwing the soil up evenly on either side— the width of the trench at the top should be at least 6 inches narrower than the spread of the cloches used.   Composted vegetable refuse should be put in the trench so that when it is trodden down it is at least 3 inches thick.   This should be forked into the bottom of the trench and well trodden down again, putting 3 or 4 inches of good soil over the top or else the John Innes Compost already described.   The trench should now be about 6 inches below the normal soil level and should be covered with cloches, making sure to seal the ends of the cloche row with large sheets of glass.   The tomatoes can be planted in ten days' time.

Soil Moisture. If the subsoil appears to be very dry when the land is dug over in the autumn, this should be well watered. When each trench is dug out it may be filled with water which must be allowed to soak through before the next spit is dug over.   The flooding should be done after the organic matter has been dug in and before the compost or good soil goes on top.   Fill the trench with water once or twice and let it soak through, thus making certain that there is plenty of water below.

The Site. This should be where the plants are sheltered from the north and east winds—a south border is best or one with a wall or strong fence at the back. Such borders are usually very dry, so make sure that they are thoroughly flooded during digging and that there is plenty of humus in the top 3 or 4 inches.

Choosing Good Plants. The best plants for raising under cloches are those that are sturdy, short-jointed and dark green with not too many side shoots. Water the plants well the day before they are put out so that the leaves are firm and turgid. If they are in paper or peat pots the whole pot is planted and so there is no disturbance of roots. Should they be in clay pots, put the plant and the pot into the hole for two or three days before knocking out, so that the temperature of the soil in the pot and the ground round about are approximately equal.

Planting. This should be done very firmly so that the lowest leaves are at soil level, making sure that the stem is never squeezed or pinched. Remove the crocks and insert the fingers at the bottom of the ball of soil to spread the roots out a little. Never press the soil around the stem itself but make sure that the ball of soil is really firm, leaving a little depression around the plant for watering afterwards—this is called ball-watering.

Staking

Method No. 1. A wire is stretched tightly between two stout stakes, one at each end of the trench and 2 inches below the top of the cloche. A short bamboo is inserted for each plant and tied firmly to the wire, the plant being trained up the stake and then bent carefully round and trained along the wire.

Method No. 2. One stake is pushed in vertically for each plant and another at an angle of about 45 degrees, and the tops of the stakes are tied together as shown in the diagram— these are arranged so that they are just below the ridge line of the cloches.

The side growth is tied to the vertical stake and the original main stem to the sloping one. The taller the cloches used and the longer the stakes the more trusses the plant can set, and the growing points of both stems must be pinched out when they

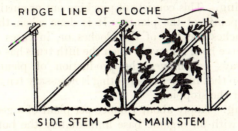

RIDGE LINE OF CLOCHE

SIDE STEM →   ← MAIN STEM

reach the top if the plants are to remain under glass coverings throughout growth.

Method No. 3. This is very much the same as Method No. 1 except that a length of fillis or string is tied to the wire and very loosely to the bottom of the plants. The string should be slightly slack so that the plant can be twisted round it as it climbs.

Method No. 4. Get the plants growing well under the cloches, using either a short stake or none at all until the glass covering is removed. Then give each one a 5-foot bamboo or string and run a top wire along about 4 feet 6 inches from soil level.

Dis-Shooting. Remove the side shoots which develop in the axils of the leaves as the plants grow—this usually has to be done once a week, at the same time removing any yellow leaves at the bottom of the plants. Cut the shoots out cleanly at their base with the tip of a sharp-bladed knife when they are just under 1 inch long. If you are going to adopt the double stem system, only one shoot should be left at the base of the plant.

Tying-In and Defoliating. The plants should be tied to the stakes immediately above a leaf, wrapping the fillis once round the string or wire and then round the stem in a loop large enough to allow for expansion ; this should be done about every 6 inches up the plant. Do not remove any of the leaves

until the fruits begin to ripen unless (a) they are turning yellow
or (b) the foliage is too thick and preventing the sun from
ripening the tomatoes. To make certain that botrytis does
not spread rub the cut end with a piece of liver of sulphur.

Stopping. This consists of pinching out or cutting out the
growing points of the plants. It is done when the growing
point reaches the top of the cloches or, in cases where the
cloches have been removed, when the fifth truss has developed.
This always encourages the production of plenty of side
growths so that further dis-shooting is necessary ten to fourteen
days after the stopping.

Feeding. Apply about 1 ounce per plant of a good tomato
fertiliser with an organic base immediately the bottom truss
has set and apply this in a ring round each plant as far as the
foliage spreads, watering it in well. A liquid manure known
as Liquinure can now be purchased for this purpose and this
contains all the plant foods in their correct proportions. A
half-strength feed is applied after each flower truss sets, giving
about half a gallon of this liquid manure per plant. This
feeding should stop after the top truss is ripening well, about a
fortnight after the setting of this truss. Some gardeners prefer
to apply Liquinure once a fortnight throughout the season at
half strength.

If the plants appear to be growing too luxuriantly, they
should be given an application of 1 ounce to the yard run of
sulphate of potash, or wood ashes at 6 ounces to the yard run
—flue dust can also be used at 4 ounces to the yard run.

Mulching and Filling-Up. Lawn mowings or soaked
horticultural peat are very good for mulching the surface of
the ground along the tomato rows, or in the bottom of the
trench when the tomatoes are being grown in this way. This
helps to keep the roots cool, and also the worms pull a great
deal of this organic matter into the ground where it will feed
the plants. Mulching should be done early in June and then
covered early in July with a 2- or 3-inch depth of surface soil
mixed with an equal proportion of peat to encourage the new
set of young vigorous roots developing from the plants.

Fruit Ripening. Plants which are stopped when they

Lantern cloches start the Tomatoes.

Note the height of the plants on June 28th as the
result of cloche coverage.

Strawberries do very well under cloches.

Raspberries can be picked a fortnight or three weeks earlier from under Tall Barns or T's.

reach the top of the cloches will have their fruit ripened without being moved. However, if the cloches have been removed, the plants can be untied and laid down at the end of September and covered with cloches to assist the ripening. First spread plenty of horticultural peat or straw on the soil and allow the plants to rest on this, afterwards cutting away most of the foliage.

Wrapping. When the cloches are removed to allow the plants to grow naturally, they can be stood up on end side by side on the north side of the plants or in a complete ring round each plant. This gives protection and also extra reflected heat to aid the ripening.

Giving Height. A good way of giving extra height to the plants under the cloches is either to use the tomato " T " cloches, or else to draw the earth up on either side of the original trench and stand the cloches on this or put boards or turves on either side on which the cloches can rest.

Extra Ventilation. The top pane of the tomato " T " cloches can be opened out a little during a very warm summer to give additional ventilation, or the barn cloches can be stood apart so that there is a 1-inch space between them. If the sun is very hot in the south-west, the cloches should be sprayed with a little lime wash to prevent sun scorching.

Pollination, Sprinkling and Watering. There is little trouble with pollination as the insects which do this work like to get under the cloches—they can always find a tiny crack by which to enter. Syringe the plants during the middle of the day with tepid water—this helps the pollen to germinate properly, and spraying the plants helps to distribute it. Do this work from either end of the rows with plenty of force. Many blossoms drop off each year through dryness at the roots so make sure that, when waterings are given after the trusses have set, the plants are soaked. A good mulching after the watering helps to conserve the moisture.

Picking. Gather the fruits when they are slightly unripe— when they are red but still firm. Lift them up carefully so that they come away from the " spur " easily with the calyx on them and a short stalk. Do not on any account squeeze the fruits or else they will bruise.

D

" Raising " the Cloches. A good method of doing this work is to have four lengths of metal rod or stout wire, each 2 feet long for every cloche. A double hook is made in one end of the rod and the other is pushed into the soil about 1 foot deep, hooks outwards, as close as possible to an eaves wire hook. With the four rods in position, raise the cloche and set it in the four rod hooks so that it is about 12 inches from the ground. This space is then filled in with glass 12 inches high and should be pushed up into the hook when it will be quite firm. It is possible to use glass 15 or 16 inches high, as the rods need not be so deep as 12 inches in the soil.

Varieties

Harbinger. A very early standard variety of excellent flavour and quality.

Hundredfold. Another good early with firm flesh and fine flavour.

Stonor's M.P. Ripens early and is a good cropper. To get the full flavour the fruits should be left on until really ripe.

Stonor's Exhibition. A heavy cropper of good flavour and firmness but the skin is rather tender.

Essex Wonder. Not a very well-shaped tomato but the flavour is good and the flesh firm. It is very easy to look after.

CHAPTER XII

HERBS

HERBS are important crops to grow, for dishes served without herb flavouring are not particularly palatable. A nice parsley sauce can make all the difference to a meal.

It is not the purpose of this book to extol the virtues of herbs, but those who do realise their importance will find the use of continuous cloches invaluable. They make it possible, for instance, to have fresh parsley all the year round. They can force mint along so that it is ready for use a month earlier than from outside pickings.

PARSLEY

Seeds often germinate slowly when sown in the open. Some people regard parsley as a difficult crop to grow, but difficulties disappear when continuous cloches are used.

Soils and Manures. Parsley will grow on almost any soil, but heavy clays should be opened up by forking in sand, flue dust or other such gritty material. Always give the surface of the ground a dressing of lime at 3 or 4 ounces to the square yard before sowing the seed.

Dig in well-rotted organic matter, 7 inches down or so, so that there is plenty of moisture-holding material there. Fork into the top 2 or 3 inches a good organic fertiliser at 3 to 4 ounces to the square yard.

Sowing the Seed. Sow the seed *very* thinly, $\frac{1}{2}$ inch deep. It makes a good edging plant. Those who want several rows should have them 1 foot apart.

The best times of sowing are early March and early August. In the former case the cloches should be put into position a fortnight beforehand, to warm the soil. In the latter case the cloches may be put over immediately after sowing.

It is possible, too, to sow as late as September, if necessary, and, in fact, almost every month during the summer, but if two good sowings are made as suggested, there should be no difficulty in keeping up the supply all the year round.

Thinning. It is most important to thin early, before the plants get overcrowded. The thinning should be carried out to 6 inches apart.

Firm the ground well after thinning. It cannot be over-emphasised that parsley likes firm soil.

Cutting Down. If the plants tend to get coarse they should be cut down, and the young growth which then comes up will be green and tender. Such hard cutting generally defers the flowering which does so much harm to the plants.

Keeping the Row Going. It is possible, by the use of continuous cloches to keep a row of parsley going satisfactorily for two years. To do this it is necessary to cover the rows with cloches from November to early April.

Before covering at the beginning of November, part of the row may be cut down early in October, and this will provide plenty of young shoots in the spring. The rest of the row may merely have some of the older leaves removed.

Varieties

Myatt's Garnishing. Long leaf-stalks, heavy cropper.
Champion Moss-curled. Very dark green, tightly curled leaves.

MINT

There are many kinds of mints available, the true spear-mint being the most useful for mint sauce. It is, however, susceptible to mint rust. The variety *Rotundifolia* is not so susceptible to rust, but some people dislike its hairiness.

Soils and Manures. A damp situation seems to suit mint best. Almost any soil will do and any odd corner. A shady border is often used with success.

Planting. A mint bed should not remain down more than two years, and it is better to replant every year.

Naturally, if the earliest mint is required, a warm, sheltered position is advisable.

Divide up the plants in March, and plant them out 6 inches

apart in the rows, so that they can be covered with cloches when necessary.

In cases where rust is bad, wash the roots well before planting out, putting them afterwards in warm water at exactly 120 degrees F. for 20 minutes.

Special Forcing. It is possible to dig up the roots of mint early in November and, having washed them well, to cut them up into portions not more than 1 inch long. These cut portions may then be planted thickly ½ inch deep in strips of sufficient width to be covered by the size of continuous cloches available.

The cutting up and covering with cloches, together with the sealing of the ends of the cloche rows with sheets of glass, cause quick growth, and mint may be produced a month or more earlier than in the normal way.

Winter Treatment. Cut the stems down hard in November, putting the cloches into position. To provide additional warmth cover the bed with a layer of straw beforehand. Close up the ends of the cloches, and excellent mint shoots will be ready to cut early in March.

SAGE

Although it is possible to raise sage from seeds, it is always better to buy cuttings or plants. Plants raised from seed soon go to seed themselves.

Soils and Manures. As advised for parsley.

Cuttings. These should consist of strong side-shoots, which should be removed with a heel of old wood in April or May. There is no difficulty in rooting such cuttings in sandy soil, covered with continuous cloches. Shade the cloches until the cuttings have fully rooted.

Planting Out. Plant out in rows 2 feet apart and the plants 2 feet apart in the rows. Cover with cloches if necessary, removing these early in June. Cover again in mid-October.

Replanting. Aim at replanting sage rows every four years.

Varieties

Broad-leaved Green. The better type.
Red Sage. Has violet-coloured leaves. Not very popular.

THYME

Thyme is very useful for flavouring soups and stews.

Propagation. It is always better to raise plants by division of roots in March and April, or by cuttings taken in September. It is possible to raise them by sowing seed, but plants thus raised are apt to flower too much, and then their flavour is not so good. Take cuttings in a similar manner to sage.

Soils and Manures. As advised for parsley.

Planting. Thyme may form an effective edging to a border, and will grow in dry borders where parsley will not do so well.

Make the rows 2 feet apart, with the plants 18 inches apart in the rows. Replant every three or four years, to prevent the plants becoming leggy.

Covering. Put the cloches into position early in October, to give protection throughout the winter.

Varieties

Common Thyme. The usual variety.
Lemon Thyme. Has a more "lemony" flavour.

CHIVES

This is another plant that may be used as an edging to a border. It provides a mild onion flavour. The shoots may be pulled all the year round.

Soils. As advised for parsley.

Planting. Propagate by division early in the spring, and plant 8 inches apart. If there is more than one row, have them 1 foot apart.

Covering. Cover about mid-September, thus keeping the chives going throughout the winter. If necessary apply a little nitrate of soda along the rows early in the spring, to start them growing vigorously again. It is a good idea to cut down half the row of chives in July so as to ensure fresh growth, then the other half of the row in September.

CHAPTER XIII

THE MORE UNUSUAL VEGETABLES

As a nation the British are very conservative about their food, and there are many vegetables which are comparatively un-known, or which are thought too difficult to grow in the normal garden.

Asparagus, with which the chapter opens, is supposed to be the rich man's crop, but actually it is not difficult to grow, especially with the help of continuous cloches. It makes a nice change, too, in the early spring.

ASPARAGUS

Cloches are used with asparagus to encourage the plants to crop earlier. They cannot, of course, turn poor plants into strong healthy ones. It is necessary, therefore, to follow the usual instructions given in regard to the growth of this crop.

Soils and Manures. Asparagus may remain in the ground for 20 years, so it is well worth while spending some time on soil preparation. One barrowload of well-rotted manure or composted vegetable refuse should be incorporated into 4 square yards. This digging should be done in the autumn, the soil being left rough to weather.

Early in March, as soon as the ground is fit to work, fork the soil over, adding fish manure or some similar organic fertiliser at 4 to 5 ounces per square yard. Finally, dress the surface of the ground with hydrated lime at 4 ounces to the square yard.

Planting. Although asparagus can be raised from seed, most people prefer to purchase plants to save time, for it is four years from the time of seed-sowing before you can take a crop.

Buy a good strain of asparagus such as " K.B." For covering with cloches, plant during the first two weeks of April, in ground that has been well prepared and is quite free from perennial weeds. Arrange the rows 36 inches apart. Choose showery weather if possible, and on no account expose the roots for a long period. Spread the roots out in spider fashion, and do not cover the crowns with more than 3 inches of soil.

General Notes. Keep the beds free from weeds by hoeing and some hand-weeding. During the summer give dried blood at 2 ounces to the square yard once every two months. Every spring give a dressing of bone meal at 4 ounces to the square yard and sulphate of potash at 1 ounce to the square yard.

Every autumn cover the beds with a 2-inch thickness of strawy farmyard manure or compost. Each January remove the surplus litter and cover the bed with $1\frac{1}{2}$ inches of soil. It is then that the fertilisers may be applied, and a week later the rows may be covered with continuous cloches.

Harvesting. Do not cut sticks the first year after planting, but every succeeding year after this cut the sticks as they appear, 3 inches below ground level, taking care not to damage the crowns of the plants. When plants are growing under cloches discontinue cutting about the middle of June.

As soon as the foliage turns yellow in the autumn, it should be cut down and burnt.

Varieties

K.B. The pedigree asparagus with the heaviest yields of large delicious sticks.

Early Argenteuil. An early variety bearing large, shapely, pointed buds, tinged with pink. An English selection of this type would appear to be **Reading Giant.**

Connover's Colossal. Has slender, pointed buds, heavy cropper.

ARTICHOKES, CHINESE

This is a good crop to grow under cloches, for the plants appreciate the extra warmth given. Pure white tubers are produced in abundance, and should be used from November to April, either in salads or cooked. The roots are delicious eaten raw, fried or boiled. The plant grows only 18 inches high, and so is quite suitable for the tent type of cloche.

Soils and Manures. Choose a well-drained, free-working soil. Light soils should be improved by the addition of plenty of organic matter, while heavy soils should be lightened by the addition of sand or other inert material such as flue dust.

Before planting, fork into the ground a good fish manure or some other fertiliser with an organic base giving a complete analysis at 4 to 5 ounces to the square yard.

Planting. This should be done in April, in drills 6 inches deep. The rows should be 18 inches apart, and the tubers placed 9 inches apart in the rows. Choose an open, sunny situation.

General Notes. Cover with cloches immediately after planting. Leave the cloches in position until the end of June, when they may be used for some other crop if necessary.

Harvesting. Lift the tubers about the third week of October and store in soil or sand in a shed, to prevent the tubers from shrivelling. When lifting, all the roots that have formed should be removed. It is important to keep them covered to preserve their whiteness. They may be left in the ground if preferred, to be dug up when required.

CAPSICUMS

Capsicums have been described as long, queerly-shaped tomatoes. They are used for flavouring pickles, for putting into salads or for cooking in soups or stews. Capsicums need plenty of water in the early stages.

Soils and Manures. The soil may be prepared as for tomatoes, and manuring may be carried out in a similar manner.

Sowing the Seed. The plants may be raised by sowing seeds under cloches as advised for cucumbers (see page 87).

Planting. The plants should be put out in their permanent positions 2 feet 3 inches apart, 15 inches apart in the rows. They may be grown under tomato " T " cloches nearly the whole time, as they never grow as tall as tomatoes. The actual planting outside should be about mid-May.

General Notes. Capsicums will not stand moisture on the foliage.

D*

Harvesting. Pick regularly as the fruits ripen. Gather the whole crop before the end of October. When you grow them without cloches you have to gather before the end of September.

CELERIAC

Celeriac grows like a turnip, and yet tastes just like the delicious hard heart of celery. It is excellent when sliced in salads or when cooked. The vegetable will keep for six months after it is fully grown.

Soils and Manures. As for beetroot (see page 47).

Propagation. As for celery (see page 70).

Planting Out. Planting may be done in May or early June in rows 18 inches apart, the plants being 12 inches apart in the rows.

General Notes. Celeriac has proved a gross feeder, so be prepared to give a liquid manure, such as Liquinure, from the end of June onwards, if possible once a week. Shallow drills may be drawn out on either side of the rows of cloches, and this liquid may be poured liberally down these drills, thus reaching the roots.

The plants may be grown under continuous cloches from the beginning, and if tent cloches are used to start with, these should be replaced by taller barn cloches about mid-July.

Harvesting. A fortnight before the hearts are to be lifted —say late October or earlier—the soil should be hoed well up to the foliage, to cause the upper part of the root to become blanched. There is no need to put the cloches back again after this.

Another method which has proved quite successful is to remove the cloches, whitewash the inside and replace them for a fortnight. The ends of the rows have to be closed, of course, so as to keep out the light.

It must be understood that this blanching is not vitally necessary, but it ensures that the whole of the root is good.

The roots may be dug up and stored in soil in a shed, or in ' buries " or " clamps " outside. In the south of England it is possible to leave them outside and use them as required, and in this case it is better to leave the continuous cloches over them.

Varieties

Paris Amélioré. A good white variety ; throws a large bulb.
Erfurt. Produces a smaller bulb of first-class quality.
Giant Prague. A good keeper, large, very solid.

EGG PLANT (AUBERGINE)

Aubergine is a very delicious vegetable when cooked, and may be stuffed and baked, cut into slices and fried or even served boiled. It makes an excellent breakfast dish when fried.

Soils and Manures. As for tomatoes (see page 92).

Sowing the Seed. As for tomatoes (see page 91).

Planting. Plant under cloches as advised for tomatoes, in a sunny situation, a south border being very suitable. Arrange the plants 18 inches apart in 2-foot rows.

General Notes. Grow the plants on a single stem from the beginning, and when they are strong enough pinch out the growing point to make them branch. Allow six shoots to form, and after this stop the side-growths by pinching them.

Like capsicums, they are apt to be attacked by red spiders, so syringe them over with warm water occasionally in the evening, taking care to avoid damping off. Much of this can be done from the ends of the rows of cloches without removing them, or if the rows are long it may be necessary to remove occasional cloches to syringe underneath. Those who have cloches with removable sides should of course take these out.

From the end of July onwards the plants will grow in the open, especially in the south.

Varieties

Purple Fine quality, large fruit, round, purplish.
Noire de Pekin. Dark violet fruit, long in shape.
Blanche Longue de la Chine. The long, white aubergine of delicious flavour. Contains more " meat " than the other varieties.

PEAS, ASPARAGUS

This is a very fascinating little pea to grow, and looks more like a vetch than an ordinary pea. It does not climb, but grows 18 inches high in a bushy form and bears masses of beautiful dark red blossoms which makes it most attractive.

Soils and Manures. As for ordinary peas (see page 57).

Sowing the Seed. Sow the seeds under cloches in early March, where the plants are to grow. They grow quite well in a south border. If more than one row is needed the next should be 18 inches away. The seed is small, so the drills need be no deeper than ½ inch.

Cover the ground where the seeds are to be sown with the continuous cloches a fortnight beforehand.

General Notes. In dry weather water well in little drills drawn out on either side of the cloche rows.

Harvesting. Pick regularly directly the pods are about 1½ inches long. If they are left on longer they get coarse. The pod is cooked as well, they are served whole and are very delicious.

SWEET CORN

Soils and Manures. Sweet corn will grow well on almost any type of soil, providing it is neither too heavy nor too light. It is probably best grown on land which has been well manured for a previous crop, for to dig in fresh dung or compost just before sowing sweet corn is apt to send the plants to leaf. Of course, on light, hungry land it will be necessary to dig in some organic matter. In all cases work half a bucketful of damped horticultural peat per square yard into the top 3 inches, together with a good fish manure, meat and bone meal or hoof and horn meal, at 3 to 4 ounces to the square yard.

Sowing the Seed. Sweet corn should never be transplanted. Sow the seed under cloches during the second week of April, or, in the north, delay until the end of April. Draw the drills 1½ inches deep, and space out the seeds at 9 inches apart in the case of Canada Cross and 12 inches apart with the taller varieties. A distance of 2 feet should be allowed between the rows. After sowing, cover with cloches, and close the ends of the rows with a sheet of glass. When the plants get too tall, the cloches may be removed and the sweet corn will develop well in the open.

General Notes. Always give sweet corn full sunshine and, if possible, arrange the crop in a block rather than in one or two rows, as this gives a better chance of pollination. There is no evidence that the removal of side shoots is an advantage. In dry weather water well, or mulch with damp horticultural peat.

Harvesting. After fertilisation, the grains pass through a watery, then a milky, and finally a doughy stage. The cobs are ready for eating at the milky stage. This is usually three and a half weeks from the time that flowering commences. The " Silks " should then be withered and brown. To find when this stage is reached, part of the sheath of a cob should be pulled back and one of the grains pressed with the thumbnail. The contents should spurt out and have the consistency of clotted cream. Always use sweet corn as soon as possible after picking.

Cooking. Strip off the husks, put the cobs in boiling water with a pinch of salt for ten minutes, pour off the water and serve hot with a smear of butter or margarine plus pepper and salt to taste.

Varieties

Canada Cross. The earliest and best, ready the third week of July.
Fogwill's Extra Early. A good early variety.
Kourtland Golden Standard. Taller, later, but quite sweet.
Golden Bantam. Very hardy, medium-sized, bright yellow.

SOYA BEANS

These are a particularly valuable crop, because the beans may contain 40 per cent. protein, 20 per cent. fat and many vitamins, especially A and B, and they also contain a certain acid which is indispensable for making new cells in our bodies.

It is a crop that is ideal for continuous cloches, for outdoors in England without any cloche covering summer nights may not be warm enough. The beans do best if their minimum night temperature is about 55 degrees F.

Soils and Manures. As for French beans (see page 54).

Situation. Soya beans seem to do best on a north border, for they are what is known as short-day plants and prefer a short sun day to a full day of sun.

Sowing the Seed. Sow the seed in exactly the same way as French beans—the same distance apart, remembering that the plants grow 2 feet in height. To get the best results, keep the plants covered with cloches of the barn type until harvesting time. It is possible, of course, to start with tent cloches till the plants grow too tall for these.

The beans can be grown in a shallow trench. Thus the cloches are given extra height, and, further, the plants when young have more shade when they need it.

Harvesting. The pods may be picked when young and the beans thrashed out green and used as green peas, or the pods may be left on the plants to ripen fully, when the beans may be thrashed out and used as haricot beans. In both cases the flavour is unique.

CHAPTER XIV

FRUITS UNDER CLOCHES

IT is not necessary, of course, to grow apples and pears under continuous cloches, but these glass tents are not too low for the normal cultivation of plums and peaches, and in fact cordon apples and pears have been grown under cloches when trained parallel to the soil.

The two fruits that can, however, be grown under cloches with advantage and success are strawberries and raspberries, although, if necessary, there should be no difficulty in growing blackberries, loganberries and similar cane-fruits, providing they are specially trained along low wires.

The obvious advantages of using continuous cloches are that protection can be given against frosts, which can easily ruin a strawberry crop for instance, and that the fruit concerned will be ready to pick from a fortnight to a month before the ordinary outdoor crops.

STRAWBERRIES

Strawberries were one of the first crops to be grown on a commercial scale under continuous cloches. As a result, the fruit ripens during the second or third week of May, according to the locality and season. Fruit growers are thus able to get the berries on to the market at a time when the highest prices can be realised.

Soils and Manures. Strawberries prefer a deep, free-working loam. Early strawberries do best on a light soil rather than a heavy one, and the market grower likes to use a soil with plenty of organic matter present. Different varieties prefer different soils—Royal Sovereign, for instance, likes a light soil and Joseph Paxton does well on heavier land. There are Cambridge Seedlings to suit all soils. Care should be taken to see that the soil never gets waterlogged at any time of the year.

Farmyard manure or good compost should be incorporated into the soil between the rows every winter. In addition, more concentrated organic manures may be given. Meat and bone meal or a good fish manure may be applied along the rows just before blossoming time, at the rate of 2 or 3 ounces per yard run. Early each autumn sulphate of potash should be given at 2 ounces per square yard. If the land is particularly light, give steamed bone flour in addition, at the rate of 3 or 4 ounces to the square yard. This may be applied at the same time as the fish manure.

Before planting, dig in a dressing of well-rotted dung or compost at the rate of, say, one good barrowload to 8 square yards, and the sulphate of potash together with the meat and bone meal, as advised above, may be forked into the top 6 inches of soil about a fortnight before planting. If it is not convenient to apply the top dressing just before blossoming, this may be put on about the end of February, just before covering the rows with cloches.

Planting. Maidens obtained from virus-free plants should always be used. Plant in August preferably, or early September, rather than in October or early the following spring.

Plant with a trowel, not with a dibber, making a hole large enough to spread out the roots. The soil should be free-working and strawberries should never be put into the ground when the soil is either too wet or too dry. Firm planting is essential, and care should be taken not to bury the crown of the plant.

When planting to cover with continuous cloches, the rows should be planned to fit in with the scheme.

Method No. 1. Arrange the rows 22 inches and 42 inches apart alternately. Put the plants in 9 inches apart in the rows. By this scheme an adequate pathway is left between every two rows of large tent cloches.

Method No. 2. Put the plants in double rows, allowing 8 inches between the rows and 12 inches between the plants. Space the double rows 24 inches and 42 inches apart.

Method No. 3. Cover single rows, planted normally, with low barn cloches.

General Notes. If rows of strawberries can be covered with continuous cloches from January onwards, the earliest

ARRANGEMENT OF STRAWBERRY ROWS FOR CLOCHE CULTIVATION

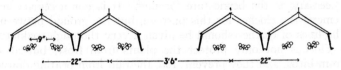

crops result, for the roots are warmed and the whole plant starts to grow six weeks or so earlier than those outside.

If, however, the continuous cloches are in use over some other crop—say lettuces—then the cloches should be put into position in March, and even then the strawberries will be picked two to three weeks before those outside.

Those who intend to force one-year-old plants may plant single rows under cloches with the plants 6 inches apart. Every other plant should be taken out at the end of the first year.

Intercropping. Winter lettuce can be grown as a catch-crop between strawberries. The procedure is to sow or plant out the lettuce in the early autumn and to cover with cloches in early October. The crop " matures " in time for the cloches to be placed over the strawberries in February, the lettuces being grown as a catch-crop between the rows of strawberries.

To ensure that the cloches are in a straight line, it is a good plan to put down a garden line first of all and line up with that. The cloches should be touching, but an extra piece of glass should be supported at the end of each row to exclude cold air.

Towards the beginning of May the cloches may be spaced out a little, leaving a gap of $\frac{1}{2}$ inch between them, so as to ensure greater ventilation. Opportunity may be taken at this time to remove weeds, stir the soil lightly and to apply the manure and add the fish manure, if this has not been done in February.

A top dressing of horticultural peat should be given while the blossom trusses are still erect. It is advisable at this time. too, to spray the inside of the cloches with a light whitewash flecking. This does not prevent the fruit from ripening properly, but protects it from sun-scorch.

As strawberries contain 80 per cent. water, irrigation is necessary as the berries are forming. It is not necessary to remove the cloches for this purpose, but the ground between the lines of cloches should be given a very thorough soaking.

Cloches not only protect the plants from frost, but also from birds, and they prevent, too, the rain from beating down on them. Thus beautifully clean berries are ensured, with the real " outdoor " flavour.

Harvesting. Pick the berries immediately they are ripe, to give the other berries a chance to swell out. Try to pick early in the day, and during very hot weather gather twice a day. After all the berries have been picked, the cloches may be removed and the peat hoed in where it lies. The soil between the rows may then be forked lightly and all runners removed.

Varieties

The best variety for cloche work is undoubtedly **Royal Sovereign Malling 40.**

Cambridge 257 ⎫ Do not make too much leaf for cloche
Cambridge 173 ⎬ work. Good flavour.

King George. Another useful type.

Madame Lefebvre. Gives very early fruits, but these are not of particularly good quality.

Other varieties that might be tried if necessary are : **Waterloo, Auchincruive Climax, Cambridge 134** and **Cambridge 276.**

RASPBERRIES

With the autumn-fruiting varieties there is no difficulty in picking berries in September and early October, but the gathering of perfectly ripened, full-flavoured, large raspberries at the beginning of June, three or four weeks earlier than outdoor ones, is most unusual. This can easily be done when using continuous cloches.

Soils and Manures. Raspberries can be grown in any

deep, well-drained soil. There must be sufficient organic matter present in the ground for the roots to get enough moisture

A convenient method of training raspberries to grow under barn cloches.

during the summer season, when the berries swell and ripen. Farmyard manure or other organic matter should be applied along the rows in February to act as a mulch. In the autumn, sulphate of potash should be applied at the rate of 2 ounces to the square yard and superphosphate at 1 ounce to the square yard. If these manures are not obtainable separately, a proprietary manure should be used which will give potash and phosphates in similar proportions.

Planting. It is most important to plant disease-free, healthy canes, and do get these early, the best time for planting being late October or early November.

Arrange the canes in rows 24 inches and 42 inches apart alternately, putting them in 1 foot apart in the rows. This ensures an adequate pathway between each double row of tall barn cloches.

Method No. 1. The newly-planted canes should be cut back to within 1 foot of the ground in February, and the rows covered immediately afterwards with tall barn cloches, taking care to close the ends of the rows with sheets of glass. Short side-shoots soon grow out, and it is these that will bear the fruit.

Method No. 2. Run a single wire for each row of canes to be planted. Strain this 10 to 11 inches from the ground from stout posts at either end of the rows. Tip the canes 6 inches or so, and train them as in the diagram above.

Method No. 3. Some time in October select healthy one-year-old canes grown on land rich in compost and plant these out just before the leaves fall, allowing 1 foot between the canes. Give a good mulching on either side of the row with damped horticultural peat just before the canes are cut down to within 15 inches of soil level in February. Put " T " cloches into position, making certain to close up the ends of the row and keep the row covered with the glass until the raspberries have been gathered. The fruit is borne on laterals which develop from the canes after they are pruned back. Incidentally, when digging up the " spawn ", as it is called, for planting out in late October, be sure to dig up as much root as possible with the cane and plant at the same depth in the new position.

General Notes. For the production of early fruits of high quality under continuous cloches it is imperative to use one-year-old plants only.

Remove any basal suckers that may appear as they will rob the strength of the main plant.

When the flowers appear, space the cloches out $\frac{1}{2}$ inch apart and spray a little whitewash with a Solo sprayer outside the cloches. This prevents the fruits being sun-scorched.

Water when the fruits are swelling, as advised for strawberries.

When all the fruit has been harvested, remove the continuous cloches, take up every other plant, and allow the row to produce its fruit in the normal manner next season.

Varieties

Malling Promise.   Huge berries with excellent flavour.
Malling Enterprise.   Very heavy cropper.
Malling Jewel.   The heaviest cropper of all.

LOGANBERRIES AND BLACKBERRIES

As has already been suggested, loganberries and blackberries may be trained along low wires and covered with continuous cloches. This brings the fruit into season three weeks to a month earlier. It is generally thought that there is not so much advantage in using cloches in the case of these two crops as there is with strawberries and raspberries.

MELONS

Melons have usually been regarded as rather a difficult crop, but under continuous cloches they have given excellent results.

They need care, of course, but then all crops do, and for the best results it is probably necessary to raise the plants in the greenhouse in pots, so that they are ready to put out at the end of May under barn cloches.

Soils and Manures. Prepare the ground by digging holes 12 inches square at stations 3 feet apart. Fill these holes with well-rotted, strawy manure or properly composted vegetable refuse ; tread down well, and then cover with 2 inches of good soil. Over the top of the hole make a mound 4 inches high and 9 inches in diameter, with soil mixed with damped horticultural peat at approximately the rate of 2 parts of soil to 1 part of peat ; when mixing, stir in 1 ounce of a good fish manure. Make these mounds in a straight line (you may only need 4 or 5 of them for the normal garden) and then cover the rows with barn cloches immediately after preparing, closing the ends of the cloche row with sheets of glass. It will be necessary to finish this work by April 11th. Leave the cloches in position for three weeks, and thus raise the soil temperature.

Sowing the Seed. Sow the seed singly in 3-inch pots in a greenhouse at the end of March or the beginning of April. The soil mixture used should consist of 3 parts good soil, 1 part horticultural peat and 1 part sand. Work into each 2-gallon bucketful of this mixture, 1 ounce of superphosphate and 1 ounce of powdered lime. Crock the pot well and fill in with the mixture, making it moderately firm only. After sowing, give a light watering and stand the pots on the staging of the greenhouse at a temperature of about 55 degrees F. Keep them growing slowly, so that on the appearance of the fifth true leaf they may be planted out on the top of the mound. This will probably be sometime in May.

Stopping and Pollination. Pinch out the growing points immediately after the fourth true leaf appears. Retain two of the resulting side-shoots (laterals), and stop them in their turn immediately above the sixth leaf. The sub-laterals which then grow out of the laterals will bear the fruit, and these sub-laterals should be stopped at two leaves beyond the little melon which has begun to swell. Non-fruiting laterals should always be stopped at the second leaf.

Pollinate the female flowers at mid-day, and do as many of them as possible on each occasion. It is usual to allow three fruits to develop on the varieties Sweet Emerald and Bellegarde, but only two on Dutch Net, Large Rock Prescott and Tiger. When the fruits start to swell they should be placed on a piece of glass to keep them off the ground.

Liquid Feeding. When the first fruits are the size of a tennis ball, liquid manure should be given every five days until ripening starts. It is quite easy to get the concentrated liquid manures in bottles to-day and to dilute them according to instructions. All watering and feeding should stop when the melons start to give forth their fragrant odour.

Watering and Ventilation. It is usually necessary to water three times a week during hot weather, and the greatest care must be taken not to let the moisture settle round the main stems of the plants, otherwise these will rot. The planting of the melons on a little mound helps towards this. Always keep the ends of the cloche rows closed until the weather gets excessively hot, and even then, before removing these ends in the day-time (they should always be put back at night-time), fleck over the tops of the cloches with some lime-wash, to break up the sun's rays and give a little shade.

Harvesting. The melons should be cut when the fruit starts to change colour and the skin starts to soften around the eye. A further indication of readiness is the little crack that appears on the skin of the fruits round the stalk. The perfume always gets stronger as the fruit gets more fully ripe. Never leave the melon on the plant until it is quite ripe. Cut it just as it is on the turn, and ripen it indoors in a dry place. You can make a melon ripen quickly or slowly according to the temperature maintained in the room in which it is being stored.

General Notes. It is always possible to apply the water outside the cloches by means of a hose or Rain King sprinkler, and to make certain that the moisture is conveyed underneath the cloches, be sure there is plenty of moisture-retaining material in the top 3 inches. This is helped by digging in plenty of damp horticultural peat round the melon mounds. Remember that melons are shallow rooters.

Varieties

Dutch Net. The best of the cloche melons. Very good flavour, mid-season, heavy cropper.

Bellegarde. Small, excellent flavour ; earliest of all. Good for late districts.

Large Rock Prescott. Larger than above; not so attractive in appearance. Late.

Sweet Emerald. A very sweet, green-fleshed, juicy, smooth melon. Not a particularly heavy cropper.

Tiger. A lovely striped melon of good flavour but not so heavy cropping as Dutch Net.

RHUBARB

Most people like to eat rhubarb early. They prefer the tender succulent forced sticks—but they may not want the bother of digging up the three-year-old roots and putting them in heat in the dark.

Cloches can be used to cause the plants to start into growth several weeks earlier than normal, providing care is taken to cover the ground with straw 6 to 8 inches deep in late December or early January. It is, of course, convenient from the cloche coverage point of view to arrange for the rows to be 2 or 2½ feet apart and to have the crowns growing at a similar distance apart in the rows.

Soils and Manures. Before planting see that the soil is well manured by digging in fully rotted farmyard manure or properly prepared compost at one bucketful to the square yard.

Rake meat and bone meal in at 3 ounces to the square yard plus sulphate of potash at 1 ounce to the square yard—or use a complete fish fertiliser. In the autumn, a feed with bottled liquid manure can be given with profit.

Lime. There is no need to lime.

Planting. Buy good crowns—these are portions split off from old plants. Set these out at, say, 2 feet by 2 feet with the top of the crown or bud buried 1½ inches below soil level. Plant firmly.

Top Dressings. Each year cover the ground where the rhubarb is growing with a 6- to 8-inch depth of straw, preferably wheat straw, and leave this in position the whole of the season.

The worms will pull it in gradually. The straw will also smother the bulk of the weeds.

Harvesting. Do not pull the first year after planting. Gather one or two sticks from each plant in the second year and in the third year force the plants by covering with cloches in late December or early January.

Varieties

Timperley Early. Perhaps the earliest kind there is.
Hawke's Champagne. Good flavour. A very popular variety with market gardeners.

VINES

As the result of the work done at the Viticultural Research Station under the direction of Mr. R. Barrington Brock, M.B.E., B.Sc., it is possible to give some very definite instructions on the subject of grape growing under cloches. Vines have been growing successfully out of doors in Great Britain for hundreds of years—certainly since the time of the Romans. It is important, of course, to grow the right varieties and to be prepared to control pests and diseases. Cloches bring outdoor vines into bearing in the third year instead of the fourth year as is the case in the open.

Soil Preparation. With vines it is important to strike a happy medium between excessive vigour of growth and the perfect ripening of the grapes. Therefore, it is not advisable to overfeed in any way. The normal digging in of one bucketful of good compost to the square yard in the autumn before planting is good practice, plus the addition of 3 ounces of bone meal, 1 ounce of sulphate of potash and 2 ounces of hoof and horn meal—all per square yard. Carbonate of lime may have to be given at from 3 to 7 ounces to the square yard depending on its pH (see page 23). It is important to cultivate the ground thoroughly prior to planting as once the vines are in, the soil should never be stirred deeper than say 4 inches.

Planting. The vines should be planted in rows 5 feet apart with the rows, say, 6 feet apart. Each vine should be given a galvanised wire stake 4 feet 6 inches above soil level and, say, 1 foot in the ground. The stakes must be joined to one another by a galvanised wire which should be stretched tightly 18 inches above soil level.

Mulching. It is not advisable to mulch in the winter because it prevents the soil's radiated heat from doing its work in preventing serious damage by spring frosts, while it is important also to get the soil to give out as much warmth as possible in the summer when the grapes are ripening.

Pruning. The best method of pruning is undoubtedly that advocated by Dr. Guyot which appears so clearly in the No. 1 Report of the Viticultural Research Station, Oxted, Surrey. I have had permission from the Director, Mr. R. Barrington Brock, to quote extensively from this report and I am very grateful to him for allowing me to do so.

The drawings on page 122 show the method clearly. The actual points where the growths are pruned are marked and the growths which develop from this pruning are seen. At the end of the third year the two branches which are retained should be 5 feet long if they are to be of sufficient vigour to bear the following season. Note in Figure IV how one shoot has been cut back to two buds and the other to eight buds. The long shoot is to be allowed to crop and the growth that has been pruned back hard will provide the necessary replacements.

In Figure V you see the replacements growing, tied up to the galvanised rod provided, and they are pruned back when they get to the top. The laterals from the other shoot are pruned at two leaves above each bunch of grapes. This summer pruning above the bunches of grapes must be done just as these bunches come into flower, for it has been shown that this assists in the setting of the blossoms.

In subsequent years the whole of the old fruiting wood is cut away, one of last year's shoots is pruned back hard within two buds of its base and the other shoot is trained out as before, being cut back to about 8 or 9 buds. Year after year this is repeated.

Do not expect more than seven or eight bunches of fruit per rod of vine, that is to say, anything from 6 to 10 pounds weight.

The rod, therefore, that is to bear this fruit should never be longer than 3 feet 6 inches and preferably should be kept to about 3 feet.

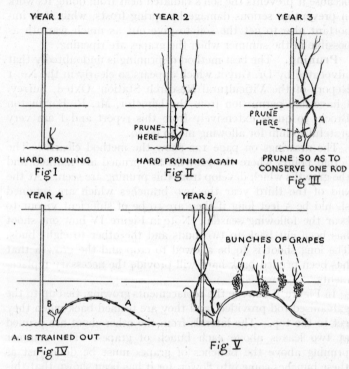

This is the ideal way of pruning. The drawings are similar to those in the No. 1 Report of the Viticultural Research Station, Oxted, Surrey (of course the bunches of grapes only appear in the summer!)

Thinning. Many varieties need hardly any thinning at all, so wait a year or so before you start worrying about this operation.

Type of Cloche. It is necessary to order a special type of " T " cloche for growing vines—this the firm concerned will supply—it is in fact the old type of narrow tomato cloche with the top glass shortened by 2 inches. This allows the galvanised rods to protrude through the top of the cloche as well as the upright summer growths when they develop. The bottom wire, of course, runs through the middle of the cloches from end to end.

Under cloches, the rod which is to bear the fruit should always be pegged to the ground as shown in the drawings on page 122. It is sometimes necessary to put a piece of glass on the ground below a bunch of grapes to prevent this actually resting on the soil. It is necessary also to remove the front glass from time to time to carry out the summer pruning. This, however, is not difficult to do in the case of the " T " cloche.

Disease Control. Powdery mildew and downy mildew may give trouble, and under cloches it is advisable to use a mixture of fine sulphur dust and powdered copper-lime dust. If these are puffed vigorously in at the ends of the cloches to produce a cloud, it will be found that this will travel 7 or 8 feet. Dusting may have to be done every six weeks in some seasons and this is another reason why it is necessary to be able to remove the front panel. Remember, however, that as the dust travels a considerable distance, the glass will only have to be removed at, say, every fourth cloche to ensure that efficient dusting is carried out. There are firms which supply special dusts for the purpose and I shall be pleased to put readers in touch with them if they cannot obtain the dusts locally.

I find it very difficult to teach newcomers how to differentiate between the powdery mildew and the downy mildew and, in fact, even experts cannot do so without a microscope. A simple plan is to treat a vine with a fine sulphur dust the moment mildew is seen and if this doesn't cure the trouble within 48 hours, to use copper-lime dust instead. I hope, however, that only the mixed dusts will be necessary. Look underneath the leaves of the vine for patches of blight—you can usually tell when they occur by a somewhat curled appearance of the leaves.

Varieties

The following varieties have proved useful when grown under cloches. They are divided into three groups, the early, mid-season and late.

EARLY :

Madeleine Royale. A white, not a muscat flavour but sweet, produces a good size white berry. Usually ready in August.

Pearl of Czaba. A very early white, has a muscat flavour and produces a good size berry. Is claimed by some not to bear heavily enough. Usually ready in August.

Sucré de Marseilles. The earliest of the black grapes, nice muscat flavour, heavy cropper. Late August.

MID-SEASON :

Chasselas Rose. A medium berried white grape of first-class flavour. The berries are tinged with red. A regular, heavy cropper.

Golden Chasselas. Very similar to Chasselas Rose but the berries are golden in colour ; very highly recommended. Both the Chasselases have the great virtue of hanging ripe under cloches until Christmas.

LATE :

Muscat Hamburgh. Large bunches, black grapes, excellent muscat flavour ; ripens late September, early October, may last with cloche protection for two months longer. Berries set rather loosely so little thinning is necessary.

White Frontignan. Produces a small berried white grape ; excellent muscat flavour ; strongly recommended. Can be picked about the same time as Hamburgh.

Summer Pruning. Mr. Barrington Brock has discovered that it is possible to open the side panels of the cloche on the ventilating wires which are provided for the purpose from the middle of June onwards, and if the fruiting shoot is trained forward a little, the tips of the laterals bearing the bunches may protrude through the ventilating slots.   Then immediately the topping takes place (see page 121), side shoots develop at the base of every leaf, and by the old method these in their turn used to be shortened.   Mr. Brock's new method is to allow the side shoots to reach a length of 3 to 6 inches and then to snap the side shoots off at their base rather like dis-shooting tomatoes.   He, in fact, calls it the de-shooting method.   Any new side shoots which develop outside the cloche may be shortened back in the normal way to, say, two or three buds, but, as a matter of fact, a certain amount of foliage outside a cloche does very little harm.

The whole advantage of this new system is that it makes the removal of the front glass a piece of work which only need be done, at the most, three times during the entire season—in fact, much less often than when growing tomatoes. An interesting point is that it is much easier to control diseases with dusts when there is less foliage inside the cloche.

PEACHES

Peaches and nectarines have been grown under the tall tomato "T" cloches very successfully for many years now. The trees are planted in a trench which is specially prepared 9 inches deep and this gives the extra height needed to the cloches. They are planted 6 feet apart and trained on wires stretched between posts, especially for the purpose. Three wires are generally used, the first 6 inches above the normal soil level, that is to say, 1 foot 3 inches above the bottom of the stem of the peach which is in the trench. The next wire is 12 inches above normal soil level and the third wire 6 inches higher still.

The trees are trained in the fan method but there is no reason to put the cloches into position until the trees have been in the ground for two years. The cloche coverage is badly needed from the middle of March until the end of May so as to give the perfect protection against frosts. If it is desired, the cloches may be removed in June for some other purpose and put back to protect the fruits from birds as they are ripening. Some gardeners like to keep the cloches in position all the time and so get much earlier peaches and nectarines.

The Peregrine peach does well under this system, as does Hale's Early. My favourite nectarine is Early Rivers. Be sure to remove the cloches in the winter so that the normal tar distillate washing can be given, using a 5 per cent. solution, and be prepared to spray with colloidal copper just as the buds are moving sometime in February. This will ensure that there will be no trouble with the peach leaf curl disease.

CHAPTER XV

FLOWERS

Continuous cloches were used in wartime entirely for vegetables, but no book on cloche gardening would be complete
without a chapter on flowers. Continuous cloches are useful
in the flower-garden not only for raising plants, but also for
covering tender specimens or for forwarding flowers.

This chapter deals with the best ways of using continuous
cloches and with the various types of flowers which have
responded well to cloche treatment.

ANNUALS

Continuous cloches are admirably suited to the annual, for
they ensure (i) successful germination of seed, (ii) the healthy
growth of the seedling and (iii) natural and adequate protection.

Soils and Manures. It is difficult, naturally, to be arbi-
trary in this connection, but as a general rule a light loam suits
annuals best. It is advisable to dig the soil at least a spade's
depth, and to apply well-rotted vegetable refuse 6 inches or so
down, at the rate of one good barrowload to 12 square yards.

Damp horticultural peat should be forked into the top 2 or
3 inches.

The situation should be open and sunny, with some shelter
from the north and east winds.

Sowing the Seed. Under cloches the three main times of
sowing for annuals are February, March and September. The
September sowings are particularly satisfactory under cloches,
for the glass tents give the necessary protection from the cold
and wet winter conditions. Those who want very early
flowers may sow annuals under cloches in February, and thus
gain an advantage of from six to eight weeks. Under such

conditions the cloches must be put into position a fortnight beforehand, to get the soil into the right tilth.

A really level surface must be assured, plus fine tilth. The seed should be sown very shallowly—not more than twice its own width. Thin sowing is imperative. Cloches should be put into position immediately afterwards, the rows of annuals being arranged to fit in with cloche covering.

Thinning. The seedlings should be thinned to 2 inches apart as soon as they are large enough to handle, transplanting the thinnings if necessary under other continuous cloches. The final thinning may be to 6 or 12 inches apart, depending on the height of the annual itself. After thinning, the remaining plants should be made firm in the ground.

General Notes. The continuous cloches may be removed early in April and used for other crops.

Varieties to Grow

Alyssum. A useful edging plant for dry, poor soil.

Anchusa capensis. Blue flowers. Grows 18 inches high.

Calendula. Transplants well. Orange flowers.

Canary Creeper. A yellow-flowering creeper.

Candytuft. Excellent for autumn sowing.

Carnation. Suits light and chalky soils. Sow Chabauds.

Chrysanthemum. Various annual types. Needs the barn cloche.

Clarkia. Dainty pink flowers. Thin to 10–12 inches.

Cornflower. White, blue and mauve. Good for autumn sowing.

Eschscholtzia. Orange, red, white or yellow flowers. Suits dry, sandy soils.

Gilia. Lovely blue flowers. Best sown in spring.

Godetia. Pink flowers, similar to clarkia.

Gypsophila. A feathery annual for lightening effects.

Larkspur. Stock-flowered type best. Thin to 12 inches.

Linaria. Flowers over long period. Good for light soils.

Linum. Grow the red and yellow types.

Love-in-the-Mist. Blue-feathery—very attractive and one of the most popular annuals.

Love-lies-bleeding. Long, attractive, hanging, cord-like deep red flowers.

Lupins. Russell varieties are best.

Mallow. A long-flowerer.

Phacelia. Good blue edging plant. Sow in spring.

Poppies. Grow both Iceland and Shirley types. Raised under cloches, longer-stemmed flowers obtained.

Scabious. Sow in autumn. Various colours.

Statice. Sow in March, dry flowers for winter use.
Sunflowers. Start under cloches only.
Sweet Sultan. Sow in autumn, various colours.
Viscaria. Sow in autumn.

General Notes. Sowing dates may have to vary to suit particular districts, but the dates given in the Chart (see page 169) may serve as a general guide.

N.B.—The chart on page 169 records actual results achieved, and shows what can be done.

Remarks. Generally speaking, autumn sowings seem to be best in the second half of September and spring sowings in early March. Cloching will be necessary ten days after sowing, or even a few days before sowing if the weather is cold. De-cloching should be done when the plants reach the glass.

As the result of sowing in the autumn and covering with cloches, flowering may be expected from mid-April onwards.

HALF-HARDY ANNUALS

The following can be grown quite easily under continuous cloches in April, the seeds being sown where the plants are to flower. Thus there is no transplanting, and the growth of the plants is not checked. If transplanting is necessary, it should be done on a dull day, and after the soil has been thoroughly moistened.

When continuous cloches are available there is never any need to raise half-hardy annuals (look for the letters H.H.A. after the names of plants in a catalogue) in a greenhouse, as is usually advised.

Varieties

Ageratum. A good blue edging plant.
Asters. Sow in seed-beds in rows 4 inches apart under cloches. When four leaves have developed prick out to 6 inches square. Re-cover with cloches. Plant out in beds late May or early June.
Cosmea. Sow where to bloom, 10 to 12 inches apart.
Dimorphotheca. Sow where to flower. Brilliant South African annual.
Helichrysum. Sow where to flower. Thin to 8 inches. Dry flowers for winter use.
Ice-plant. A creeping plant with pink or white flowers.
Kochia. Sometimes called " Burning Bush ". Sow where to grow.

A wonderful Cantaloupe—easy to produce under Barn cloches.

Rows and rows of Melons.

Early annuals are useful as cut flowers.

Love-in-the-Mist on June 4th. The glass coverage
has done the trick !

Mesembryanthemum criniflorum. Sow where to flower. Thin to 12 inches apart. Likes hot, dry soils. Excellent for covering sunny bank.

Mimulus. Various coloured flowers, mostly yellows and bronzes. Likes a damp situation.

Nemesia. Sow where to flower. Blossoms orange, red, yellow, blue.

Nicotiana. Likes deep, rich soil ; sow where to flower, in February, or transplant. Often called Tobacco Plant.

Petunia. Sow and transplant. A drought resister. Lovely range of colours in flowers.

Phlox Drummondii. Various colours. Sow where to flower.

Rhodanthe. Pink or white flowers. Everlasting. Sow where to flower.

Rudbeckia. Hates root disturbance. Flowers yellow or orange.

Salpiglossis. Excellent as cut flower. Sow where to flower.

Schizanthus. Sow where to flower. Pinch out growing point to cause plants to branch.

Ten-week Stocks. Sow end February, prick out under further cloches as soon as large enough to handle. Smaller seedlings give most doubles. Water well. Shade during bright sunlight till plants have picked up. When 6 inches high, late in May or early June, plant out in permanent positions.

Ursinia. Orange, South-African edging plant.

Venidium. Sow mid-March, where to bloom.

Verbena. Likes light, dry soils. Sow late February and transplant.

Zea. Tall, decorative foliage plants. Common name, Japanese Maize.

Zinnia. Continuous cloches make all the difference to this plant. Sow mid-March. Thin seedlings to 12 inches apart.

SWEET PEAS

Perhaps the annual which gives the most pleasing results under continuous cloches is the sweet pea. Naturally, it is important to obtain good seed from a reliable source.

The seed should be sown where the plants are to grow —say, in specially prepared trenches—during the second or third week of October. A further sowing may be made if necessary during February or early March. Draw the drills out 3 inches deep, and put the seeds in 2 inches apart. In the case of the varieties with hard coats nick the seeds beforehand.

Cover with tent cloches immediately after sowing, OR, should the weather be wet, the cloches should be put into position a fortnight before seed-sowing. When the seedlings are 4 inches high, thin them to 4 inches apart, transplanting them if neces-

E

sary to other positions. If the plants are to be trained as cordons, thin to 8 inches apart. Remove the cloches the third or fourth week of March or, for extra early flowers, leave in position until the second week of April. When the plants reach the top of the cloches, the cloches must either be removed or replaced by those of larger size.

Direct sowing under continuous cloches does away with all planting out and ensures the right watering and ventilation. It is thus labour saving. It ensures that the seedlings grow sturdily and that the root system is never disturbed, and the plants thus withstand early droughts better.

Varieties

Anchusa. A clear, bright, solid mid-blue.
Albatross. Giant flowered pure white.
Reconnaissance. Cream with rose picotée edge.
Mrs. R. P. Butchart. Large, deep lavender-blue.
Mrs. C. Kay. Clear mid-lavender.
Moonlight. A giant flowered cream.
Radiant. Bright rose-flushed salmon, cream ground.
Autumn Gold. Deep rich salmon with a cream ground.
Princess Elizabeth. Salmon-pink on creamy-buff.
Patricia Unwin. Golden salmon-pink on cream ground.
Mrs. R. Bolton. Deep, rich rose-pink with a white ground.
Air Warden. Light bright scarlet.

BIENNIALS

Continuous cloches are ideal for biennials, for the plants can be sown out of doors in May or June, and can then be covered with continuous cloches in the autumn to give protection, or, if preferred, very early in the spring, to encourage early flowers.

Soils and Manures. As for annuals.

Varieties

Brompton Stocks. Sow June, July, where they are going to flower, if possible. Before sowing seed be sure to give lime at 4 ounces per square yard on surface. Arrange so that the rows can be covered with size of cloche used. Plant at least 12 inches square. It is possible to sow in seed-bed, prick out to 4 inches apart in nursery bed, and then to transplant in September where stocks are to flower.
Forget-me-nots. Sow seed mid-May in open. In October lift

plants, plant in double rows for wide barn cloches, single rows for narrow barn cloches. Plant 8 inches apart. Cover with cloches in November. Flowers will bloom late in March, early April.

Pansies. Sow seeds under cloches in March in very fine soil ; adding sand to surface soil is a good plan. Plant out seedlings in shady spot, 6 inches square. Cover with cloches in November.

Polyanthus. Sow seed in February. Put cloches in position for a fortnight beforehand. Mix seed with ten times its own bulk of sand. Sow very shallowly. Prick out in shady position when three leaves have developed. Incorporate plenty of leaf mould into ground before planting. Keep plants supplied with water during summer. Lift in October ; replant close together in rows in such a way that two rows can be covered with barn cloches early in November. Continuous supply of flowers thus available throughout winter and early spring.

Sweet Williams. Sow seed in May. Transplant seedlings 8 inches apart. Arrange plants in rows, 6 inches apart. Cover with tall barn cloches in November.

Wallflowers. Sow in open, as usual. Transplant close together. Cover with barn cloches in January. Very early flowers assured.

PERENNIALS

Most perennials are propagated by divisions or by root cuttings (see Chapter XVI). Few perennials come true from seed, but cloches can be used for raising flower seedlings just as easily as for vegetable seedlings. If the sowing is done early in the spring, the plants may flower the same year.

Soils and Manures. As advised for annuals.

Varieties for Raising Under Cloches

Alstroemeria. Sow mid-March under cloches, mixing a little mustard seed in drill. This enables weeding to be done early. Thin out seedlings when they appear—6 inches apart. When plants are two years old lift every other tuber and transplant.

Aquilegia. Sow in March very shallowly under cloches Position, semi-shade. Will flower end of summer.

Auriculas. Sow in March in fine soil under cloches. Remove cloches in summer. Replace early in winter.

Border Carnations. Choose light, well-drained sandy soil. Sow March under cloches.

Delphiniums. In areas where these perennials die out in ground in winter cover individual plants with four-sided cloches. Raise new plants by sowing seed under cloches in February or early March. These will flower in September.

Lupins. Sow as for delphiniums.

Pansies. See biennials.

Pentstemons. Sow seed in February or early March ; under cloches seedlings bloom same year.

Physalis. Sow February and March under cloches. Usually called " Chinese Lantern ".

Thalictrum. Sow March under cloches. Transplant 8 inches apart. Transplant into border early in autumn.

Herbaceous plants that appreciate covering with cloches during winter, especially in the north :

Aquilegia ; Delphinium ; Galega ; Gazanea ; Geum ; Lobelia cardinalis ; Lupins ; Mesembryanthemum ; Phlox ; Romneya ; Salvia ; Scabious ; Thermopsis ; Thalictrum.

Perennials that will bloom in winter under continuous cloches :

Christmas roses ; Winter-flowering pansies and violas ; Sternbergias ; Leucojums ; various Polyanthus ; miniature Cyclamens and various Anemones.

BULBS

This section is devoted to all bulbous plants and, in fact, all plants that may be treated in the same way, whether bulbs, corms, rhizomes or tubers.

The great advantage of continuous cloches is that they will advance the time of flowering by a fortnight or so, and protect the blooms from frost, wind and rain. The majority of the bulbs should be planted in September, so that they may have a chance of making a strong root-system.

Depth of Planting. The actual depth of planting varies with the size of the bulb. The general rule is that it should be buried its own depth. Make certain that the base of the bulb rests firmly on soil.

Distance Apart. Tulips may be planted in rows 4 inches apart, the bulbs 3 inches apart in the rows. Hyacinths, however, which spread more, need 4 inches by 4 inches.

All bulbs mentioned below should be planted in the autumn, except where expressly stated.

Varieties to Grow Under Cloches

Aconites. Cover with tent cloches in December.

Chionodoxa. Cover with tent cloches in January.

Crocuses. Cover with tent cloches as soon as buds appear. Close ends of rows with sheets of glass.

Daffodils. Cover with tomato " T " cloches in November. Close ends of rows with sheets of glass.

Hyacinths. Plant early October. Cover with cloches in November. When flowering spike develops, lift if necessary and transplant in bowls.

Irises. Cover *Iris reticulata, histrio* and *histrioides* in January. Cover *Iris stylosa* (*I. unguicularis*) in November.

Lily of the Valley. Cover with barn cloches in November. Result, long stems, flowers three weeks earlier than those uncovered. Plant in November, *firmly*. Bury tips of buds 1 inch below soil.

Muscari. Cover with continuous cloches in November. Often called Grape Hyacinths.

Scillas. Cover with continuous cloches in January.

Tulips. Cover with tall barn cloches in November. Close ends of rows.

TWO SPECIAL PLANTS

ANEMONES

Soils and Manures. As for annuals (see page 126).

Sowing the Seed. Sow beginning of February to end of March. Drills 1 inch deep, 1 foot apart. Mix seed with sand to facilitate even and thin sowing. Cover with cloches immediately. Remove cloches in April. Thin seedlings to 6 inches apart. Keep bed well hoed.

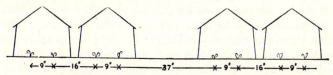

Spacing Rows of Anemones under large Barn Cloches.

Planting Tubers. For providing winter flowers, plant in June and July. Drills 1½ inches deep, tubers 4 inches apart. Convenient to arrange double rows 9 inches apart, spaced alternately 16 inches and 37 inches. This allows a 2-foot pathway between each double row of cloches.

DAHLIAS

May easily be raised from seed under cloches, particularly Coltness Gem types. Sow seed ½ inch deep and 1 inch apart in March. Cover with tent cloches. Thin seedlings to 9 inches apart.   Transplant thinnings to 6 inches apart under other cloches.   Keep cloche coverings until early June.

Sowings may be done where plants are to bloom, or seedlings may be transplanted.

Four-sided continuous cloches may also be used for covering dahlias planted early or for covering tubers planted in the border at the end of March or beginning of April.

SPECIAL NOTES ON FLOWERS FOR CUTTING

There are a number of flowers which are excellent when grown under cloches.   The blooms can be cut, say, three weeks before those growing in the open, and where growers have a good sale for flowers the cloche-covering scheme is very popular.

In many cases it is advisable to use the taller type of cloche like the "T" or to use a large barn or growers' barn with the necessary adaptors that will lift them up another foot off the ground on the wires provided together with the glass side panels.   By giving extra height in this way it is possible to keep the cloches over the taller types of perennials, annuals and bulbs much longer.

If cloches are to be used for this purpose, the rows will have to be planted so as to fit in with the cloche coverage.   With bulbs, there's no difficulty in the rows being 4 inches apart and the same kind of rule holds good for corms like the gladioli. Both bulbs and corms can then be 3 inches apart in the rows. The smaller bulbs like snowdrops could, of course, be planted even closer, say, 3 inches by 2 inches.

DAFFODILS

Plant four rows at 4 inches apart and these will just be covered with a growers' barn cloche.   Leave a space of 6 inches and have another four rows and the barn cloche lines will be running parallel to one another with the bases of the cloche lines 2 inches apart.   Then leave a space of 2 feet and have your next double row of cloches with the daffodils planted under them and as a result you will have plenty of room to pick them.

The ground on which the bulbs are to be planted will be prepared as advised in Chapter II by bastard trenching and the compost added at the same time. A good firming will be done afterwards, the bulbs then planted about 6 inches deep. Some take the trouble to sprinkle silver sand into the bottom of the hole made so that the base of the bulb rests on this. Cover the rows with cloches in November. Raise the cloches on adaptors early in March. Uncloche altogether about the third week of March.

Varieties

There are a large number of varieties that could be used but the following have been found to do particularly well under cloches and are therefore recommended:

King Alfred. A large, golden-yellow trumpet.

Helios. A scarlet cup and primrose perianth, very early.

Bath's Flame. Follows the above and is similar in colour but longer petals on the whole.

Crœsus. To follow Bath's Flame, perianth white, cup orange, petals broad.

Fortune. A huge type of Helios, very popular, but bulbs rather expensive.

Golden Harvest. A large type of King Alfred, but better colour, bulbs somewhat expensive.

TULIPS

These can be treated in almost the same manner as daffodils. The ground is prepared in the same way—they are planted in a similar manner. The best sized bulbs for cloches are 10 cm. and upwards. The great thing is to grow the Darwins and the Cottage tulips and not the ordinary Earlies.

The planting should be done in September, and the cloching in November. The raising of the cloches on adaptors should be carried out in late March, and the cloches will be available to pass on to gladioli about mid-April. Lift the bulbs in July and separate them, dry them off carefully and if there are any really good plump ones, plant them in September. Some people, by doing their tulips well, manage to save a fairly large percentage of bulbs each year, but for the best results it is a good thing to buy new bulbs each season. Experiments seem to show that it helps if Liquinure (Flower Special) is used just when the flower buds start appearing in the spring, at the rate of a gallon to the yard run, and a second feed given ten days later. This not only helps to give larger and better flowers but it also ensures a better crop of bulbs for the next season.

The main trouble with tulips is a disease known as Tulip Fire and the best control is to dust with a fine copper-lime dust. This can easily be done by removing one cloche in eight and puffing the dust down the rows with a Rotary Fan Dust Gun.

Varieties

DARWIN TULIPS :

Clara Butt. Grows to a height of 26 inches with flowers of a delicate salmon-rose with blush tinge on outer petals.

Farncombe Sanders. Rich fiery rose-scarlet flowers with clear white base. Height 30 inches.

William Pitt. Shaded carmine. Height 26 inches.

City of Haarlem. Immense vermilion scarlet flowers, best red Darwin. Height 30 inches.

Le Nôtre. Beautiful clear pink with strong stem. Height 26 inches.

Pride of Haarlem. The interior of the flower is salmon-scarlet with a blue base ; outside glossy carmine ; early. Height 29 inches.

COTTAGE TULIPS :

Inglescombe Scarlet. Brilliant red, very large flower, height 20 inches.

Prince of Orange. Orange-scarlet, edged bright yellow, height 20 inches.

Inglescombe Pink. Bright pink shading to buff and salmon. Conical-shaped flower. Height 23 inches.

Bronze Night. Rich coppery-bronze, very striking, large flower. Height 22 inches.

La Candeur. White changing to soft rose ; large globular flower.

Inglescombe Yellow. Glossy canary-yellow ; large pointed flower.

GLADIOLI

The corms of gladioli are easy to grow, but it must be remembered that they are moisture-loving plants, and therefore it is important to bastard trench and dig in well-rotted compost at a bucketful to the square yard and then to fork into the top 3 or 4 inches horticultural peat at half a bucketful to the square yard. Because the corms are going to be covered with cloches they may be planted on the 1st March —this means putting the cloches into position over the ground to warm it a fortnight beforehand.

Draw out drills 3 to 4 inches deep, plant the corms 3 inches apart in the rows with the rows 4 inches apart, as for daffodils —you will then get four rows under the large barn cloche. Many growers plant a second batch of corms about 1st July in order to get some gladioli in flower early in October—this second planting need not be covered with cloches unless the weather is very wet at planting time.

The cloches should be raised on their adaptors at the end of the first week of May and it should be possible to decloche altogether by, say, the third week of May, when the cloches can be used if desired for zinnias. It is usually necessary to support the spikes when they appear and this can either be done with individual bamboos or, better still, with strings stretched tightly along the whole length of the row, one string at 18 inches, the next at 2 feet 6 inches and maybe another at 3 feet or 3 feet 6 inches. The corms are lifted with their dead foliage in October and are usually hung upside down in a shed, and then about six weeks later it is easy to separate the corms from the dead stems and store them in a frostproof place for the winter.

There is a bacteria which may give trouble, causing the leaves to look as if they had been attacked by leaf miner. Treating the corms in a solution of Calomel for ten minutes before storing is usually a cure. Dissolve 1 ounce of Calomel in 1 gallon of water for the purpose. Spraying with colloidal copper (Bouisol) gives control if applied when the trouble is first seen in the summer.

Varieties

Baron von Wynbergen. Salmon-rose.
Dr. Dents. Salmon-pink.
Allard Pierson. Deep bright rose, shaded orange.
Bit of Heaven. Uniform orange.
Clingendaal. Cochineal-red.
Early Sunrise. Red with white blotch.
Red Fox. Dark red.
Rosa von Lima. Brilliant rose.
Ragenbogen. Salmon-carmine, yellow blotch.
Maskerade. Yellow with darker blotch.
Gold Dust. Butter-flowered yellow.
Fahrenjunker. Light yellow.
Lilac Wonder. Violet-blue.

CHRYSANTHEMUMS

I want under this heading to include the special ways in which cloches can be used for this queen of autumn flowers. Those who have not any experience of this flower will do well to study *The ABC of Flower Growing* and *The ABC of the Greenhouse* or, if they are interested in selling flowers to make money, there is *Modern Flower Growing for Profit* and its companion *Modern Glasshouse Flower Growing for Profit*.

The best chrysanthemums I ever saw were those grown by digging in by hand 75 tons of dung to the acre which is the kind of liberal treatment that the chrysanthemum likes. Bastard trench the land in the winter, add as much well-rotted dung or fully rotted compost as you can, 6 or 7 inches down, and then leave the ground rough for the frost and cold winds to act upon. In the spring, rake the land down level, apply a good fish manure at 3 to 4 ounces to the square yard, or hoof and horn meal at a similar rate plus sulphate of potash at 1 ounce to the square yard. The cloches are then put into position over the ground that is to be planted up in order to warm it. The chrysanthemums which have been raised in the greenhouse may now be planted with safety about the beginning of April, with one plant in the middle of each cloche, so that you get one long single line with the plants themselves about 18 inches apart. It's a good plan on the light soils to plant the chrysanthemums in trenches 6 inches deep like celery, and thus when the cloches go in position, the plant is ensured extra head room. This can be done on almost any soil where the drainage is perfect.

Stopping is done when the plants are about 5 inches tall—that is to say, usually late in April or early in May. Some people manage to stop earlier than this so that by the middle of May they can stop a second time. This stopping consists of pinching out the growing points with the idea of causing the buds in the axils of the leaves to break out and so form a much bushier type of plant. Another advantage of stopping is that it causes the plants to flower earlier.

By the end of May or the beginning of June the cloches can be removed. The plants will have grown tall and will look very healthy. From that time onwards the chrysanthemums will grow in the open.

It is possible also to grow the dwarf autumn-flowering varieties under the tall " T " cloches, and in this case the plants are put out in the normal way about the beginning of May in the south and towards the end of May in the north, and then protected with cloches at the end of September or the beginning of October. This is a scheme which is more successful in the south than in the north where there may be far more severe frost. Cloches will keep out 5 or 6 degrees of frost and so protect the blooms, but they can't be expected to keep out 12 degrees of frost and guarantee that the flowers are not touched.

Varieties

Good varieties to grow out of doors with initial cloche coverage are :

Imperial Yellow, Royal Pink, August Pink and that very early called **Sweetheart ; Royal Bronze, Arnhem** and **Carefree,** three bronzes ; and **Superward** and **Hurricane,** two red-crimsons. Incidentally, **Imperial Yellow** must be stopped in mid-May to get good flowers in September.

CARNATIONS

Cloches are very useful for (a) ensuring that the outside carnations flower much earlier and (b) for giving protection to the plants in the wetter districts of the country. When preparing the soil, see that clay is opened by forking in half-rotted straw or horticultural peat at the rate of a bucketful to the square yard. With light soil fork in really well-rotted compost or damped horticultural peat at a similar rate so as to ensure that the plants do not suffer from lack of moisture in the summer. Carnations like lime, so apply carbonate of lime at 6 to 7 ounces to the square yard.

Buy good named varieties (see below) and plant these at the end of September in the north and about the middle of October in the south. For cloche coverage it is ideal to plant 9 inches square. Cover the carnations with cloches at the end of October and leave them in position until March, making sure to close the ends of the cloche rows. If the stems have touched the top of the glass and the weather is still cold and wet the cloches may be raised on adaptors until, say, the end of April.

Under this scheme it should be possible to cut good carnations from the beginning of June onwards, and disbudding may be carried out to ensure large specimens. The following October the long shoots can be cut back and the plants made compact once more, and again the cloches can go into position so as to give the right kind of protection.

Varieties

BORDER CARNATIONS :

Pink Clove. The most fragrant of all the pinks.
W. B. Cranfield. Geranium-scarlet, perfect flower.
Oakfield. Clove, glowing crimson, perfumed.
Loyalty. Apricot, compact habit, good growth.
Lavender Clove. Best heliotrope, self-coloured variety.
Dainty. Primrose-yellow ground, edged and splashed with pink.
Nobility. White ground flaked with bright crimson. Large flowers.
Madonna. The best white.

COTTAGE CARNATIONS :

Cottage Crimson. Old clove perfume.
Cottage Mauve. Full flower, plant of good habit.
Cottage White. Highly fragrant.
Cottage Scarlet. Rich in perfume.
Diplomat. Salmon-pink ground specked with deep salmon.

VIOLETS

In many parts of the country excellent violets are grown under continuous cloches. The beds are prepared in April by digging in really well-rotted farmyard manure or fully composted vegetable waste at one bucketful to the square yard. In addition, horticultural peat is added at half a bucketful to the square yard and is raked into the top inch or so of soil.

The grower then takes his runner plants, either from the stock he has been growing already or he buys one-year-old runners from a reliable nurseryman. The great thing is to get these planted in May. Always choose a runner which has been produced close to the parent plant as this gives the best results.

It is quite a good plan to have the rows 9 inches apart and the plants 6 inches apart in the rows, and then to leave a space of 18 inches and have the next two rows planted in a similar manner.   As a result it is possible to cover with barn cloches when the time comes.

Cultivations.   Hoe regularly but very shallowly.   Never allow weeds to develop and never allow the plants to send out runners during the summer.   Watch out for red spider which causes the leaves to turn yellow and try and prevent the trouble by spraying the undersides of the leaves regularly with clean water.   The variety Governor Herrick is immune from red spider but is scentless.   Market gardeners often put a little violet scent on the blooms, for that reason.

Cloche Coverage.   Put some damped horticultural peat along the rows and in between the plants to act as a mulch. Cover with cloches late in October, close the ends of the cloche rows and keep them in position until about the middle of March.

Harvesting.   Pick twice a week from the middle of September until the end of March—it helps if the cloches used can have a removable panel, because the picking can then be done without having to shift the cloches bodily.

Varieties

Princess of Wales.   A lovely blue, which in the Cornish Trials was given the best marks.

Governor Herrick.   A deep purple, with a large flower but no scent.   Much liked because it is a red spider resister.

Lloyd George.   A blue with a long stem, but not quite so free flowering as Princess of Wales.

Queen Mary.   A double pale mauve, liked by cloche growers because it is such a compact grower.

Comte de Brazza.   The best double white.

Marie Louise.   A beautiful double mauve, much liked because of its good scent.

Diseases and Pests.   Violets may be attacked by a number of pests and diseases.   There's a type of greenfly, for instance, which first appears in April or May and it is controlled by spraying with nicotine, using $\frac{3}{4}$ ounce of nicotine to 10 gallons of water.   Before planting it is a good plan to dip the young violets into a solution of nicotine and a detergent like Shell Estol, to make certain that all pests are killed.

Red spider has already been mentioned and it helps tremendously if the plants can be syringed regularly. Some gardeners spray with clean water using 100 pounds pressure. White oil emulsions like Volck have given good control in bad cases—two sprayings are necessary at twelve-day intervals.

Eelworms may attack violets and become a very severe pest. It is hoped that the warm-water treatment will prevent them, and those who are interested may obtain further information from the Seale Hayne Agricultural College.

ZINNIAS

During the last three or four years zinnias have become more and more popular and they are excellent cloche flowers. They normally grow in the Middle East and they like the extra warmth. The soil should be prepared as advised for daffodils (see page 135). The seed may be sown directly under the cloches about the last week of March in the south of England and about the third week of April in the colder parts of the north. It is possible to get a double row of zinnias under the large cloches, the rows being a foot apart. The plants will be thinned to 6 or 8 inches apart when they are an inch or so high.

By the middle of May the zinnias will have reached the top of the cloches which should now be raised on adaptors, and they will remain in position with the adaptors giving the extra height and protection until, say, the end of May when they will be removed. The zinnias will flower about the third week of June and magnificent specimens will be produced.

Varieties

Rose Queen. A bright rose.
Lavender Gem. A lavender turning purple.
Pink Profusion. A delicate shrimp-pink.
Scarlet Gem. Glowing scarlet.
Orange King. A burnt orange.
Purity. A white.

CHAPTER XVI

CONVENIENT PROPAGATION

CONTINUOUS cloches are ideal for use when propagating plants vegetatively. Most plants can be raised from seed, but this in many cases is too slow for the gardener. Further, in order to obtain plants which resemble their parents in every characteristic, it is necessary to use a portion of that plant and induce it to form roots.

The use of hormone preparations such as Hortomone A (instructions are found on the packet) are a tremendous aid to immediate and excellent root formation.

CUTTINGS

Cuttings may be made in the summer or autumn. The chosen cutting or shoot should not be one which is flowering, and should be sturdy and short-jointed. When evergreen conifers are used, only the tips of terminal shoots should be taken.

The Cutting Bed. Choose a well-drained, open situation. See that it is level and incorporate plenty of silver sand. Arrange the bed so that it can be covered with two rows of cloches close together, a path and then another two rows of cloches, etc.

Cover the part over which the continuous cloches are to be placed with a ½-inch layer of coarse, gritty sand. When the original soil is very heavy, arrange for a slightly raised bed.

Putting in the Cuttings. Make cuttings a few at a time, inserting them before they wilt. Arrange the rows 3 inches apart, leaving 1 to 3 inches between each cutting, according to size. Make the cuttings firm and ensure that their bases rest on sand. Water immediately afterwards with water with the

chill off.   Put continuous cloches into position, close the ends
of the rows with sheets of glass held in position by wire.

If the weather is very sunny, shade the cloches with some
material.   Give the cuttings a light syringing with water once
a day in hot weather to prevent them flagging.

Cuttings to Take in the Autumn. Pansies ; Pent-
stemons ; Violas ; many shrubs like Veronica ; Evergreen
Conifers ; and such rock plants as Aubrietia, Arabis, Phlox,
Dianthus, Thymus, etc.

Cuttings to Take in the Summer. Gypsophila (perennial) ; Michaelmas Daisies ; Scabious (perennial) ; Phlox ;
and such shrubs as Deutzia, Philadelphus, Cistus, Spiræa.

Special Notes.

(1) With herbaceous plants, use strong, basal shoots appearing in April, May and June.

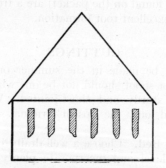

Diagram of root cuttings.

(2) With shrubs, take cuttings with a heel of old wood.

(3) Don't allow pansies and violas to flower during the
summer.   In August cut such plants hard back.   Choose
young, basal growths for cuttings.

Root Cuttings. Many plants are best propagated by root
cuttings, especially those with thick, fleshy roots.

Plants should be lifted immediately after flowering, the roots
being divided into portions, varying from 1½ to 3 inches long,
according to root thickness.   The portion of the root near the

top of the plant should be cut square, and the bottom end slanting.

Where the roots are pencil-thick or over, cuttings may be 3 inches long. Where the roots are slender, cuttings need be only 1 inch in length.

Putting the Cuttings Into Position. Choose a sunny site and see that it is well drained. Incorporate gritty sand into the top 4 or 5 inches. Make straight-sided trenches, 1 inch deeper than the length of the cutting. Place a little sand in the bottom of the trench and put the cutting in upright. Cover so that the top is buried ½ inch deep. Water well. Cover with cloches. Close up the ends of the row with sheets of glass.

Hard Wood Cuttings. It is possible to use cloches to hurry the rooting of hard wood cuttings. These may be of gooseberries, redcurrants, blackcurrants, rambler roses or a number of deciduous shrubs (the shrubs whose leaves fall each autumn). The cuttings are usually prepared by making a cut with the sharp blade of a knife just below a bud at the bottom end and just above a bud at the top end. With roses and fruit bushes the cutting may be 12 inches long and with the deciduous shrubs, say, 10 inches long. As it is advisable to have the gooseberries and redcurrants on a leg—that is to say, with a good stem—all the buds should be removed with the exception of the top three, and the cuttings then inserted 6 inches deep. It is necessary to encourage growth of blackcurrants from the base and so no buds should be removed. With shrubs, a decision will have to be made as to whether basal growths or suckers are required or not and whether to disbud or not, depending on the type of bush required.

The cuttings will be planted 6 inches from one another in rows 6 inches apart. The soil should be fairly sandy ; if this is not the case, it is advisable to take out small trenches and lay the cuttings upright in these throwing a little sand at their base. The great advantage of using cloches in this way is that early rooting is encouraged and better bushes are produced as a result in a shorter time.

CHAPTER XVII

PESTS AND DISEASES

ONE of the great advantages of continuous cloches is that plants grown under them are not attacked by pests and diseases in the same way as outdoor plants, especially if the ends of the cloche rows are closed with a sheet of glass.

The turnip-flea beetle, the carrot fly and the onion fly are three typical pests which seldom, if ever, damage their respective crops when grown under these glass tents. The reason is probably easy to find, and that is that the pests do not reach the plants as easily, as the glass covering keeps them away. Under continuous cloches, in fact, many crops are harvested before the eggs of their insect pests are laid. Thus they are out of the way before the pests can damage them.

Another great advantage is that because of the coverage of cloches, if a pest should attack it can proceed with its work in only two directions, instead of many.

Naturally, the soil pests, such as slugs, wireworms, leather-jackets, etc., are not affected by continuous cloches at all. It can be said with truth that slugs, for instance, do not like the dry surface tilth which is always found under the glass cloche, but apart from this the glass gives no special protection.

This chapter, therefore, does not deal with all the pests and diseases known to attack garden crops, but only with those that may attack crops grown under continuous cloches. There may be exceptions to the rule, but the remarks that follow are made as a result of the experience of the last ten years or more.

PESTS

Aphides

Aphides—*i.e.*, green fly, blue fly, etc.—may attack plants

under cloches, especially lettuces, peas and beans, carrots and members of the cabbage family.

They are sucking insects, and usually attack the under surface of the leaves first. They multiply at an exceedingly fast rate, and must be controlled in the early stages.

Control Measures. Spray with a good type of Liquid Derris, giving a good soaking. In the case of badly curled leaves, a nicotine spray may be advisable so that the fumes can penetrate under the curled surfaces. Formula : $\frac{1}{4}$ ounce nicotine, $\frac{1}{4}$ pound soft soap to $2\frac{1}{2}$ gallons water. Nicotine is a poison, and should be kept locked up when not in use.

Derris is not poisonous, and is safe to use at any time.

Chafer Beetles

The grubs of the chafer beetles are about $1\frac{1}{2}$ inches long, have three pairs of legs only, and are fat, white and objectionable-looking. These grubs live in the soil and eat the roots of plants.

Control Measures. When found, fork in D.D.T. dust or naphthalene at the rate of 1 ounce to the square yard. Naphthalene drives away the pests—D.D.T. usually kills them.

Caterpillars

All kinds of caterpillars are found on vegetables, flowers and fruits. They can easily be controlled if they are tackled in the early stages.

Control Measures. Spray or dust with some reliable form of Derris or use D.D.T.

Cut Worms or Surface Caterpillars

Unfortunately these are more common under continuous cloches than in the open. They seem to like the warmth ! The caterpillars are sometimes $1\frac{1}{2}$ inches long and at other times only $\frac{1}{2}$ inch long. They are usually grey or brown in colour, and wander about just above or below the surface of the ground, damaging plants by biting through their stems. They feed at night.

Control Measures. Bait with bran and Paris Green, or dried used tea-leaves and Paris Green. Formula : $\frac{1}{4}$ pound bran, 1 ounce Paris Green, pint of water ; or ¼ pound tea-leaves and 1 ounce Paris Green (no water need be added). Mix together ; sprinkle over the surface of the ground. This quantity is sufficient for ¼ acre of crops under cloches.

D.D.T. dusted on the ground will kill cut worms.

Leather-Jackets

The leather-jacket is the larva of the daddy-longlegs. In the north of England it is called the " bot ". It lives 1 or 2 inches below the surface of the soil, and in this way is able to feed on the stems and roots of plants below ground.

Control Measures. Apply bran and Paris Green bait as advised for surface caterpillars. Make application early in the evening.

Millipedes

Millipedes should not be confused with centipedes. Centipedes do good. They have flattened bodies, and each segment of their bodies has only one pair of legs. Millipedes have round bodies, the front four segments of which have one pair of legs each, while the remaining segments have two pairs of legs each.

Control Measures. Fork whizzed naphthalene into the soil at the rate of 1 ounce to the square yard. This usually drives them away.

Bury large cut carrots 1 inch deep in the ground. Spit the carrots on a stick, so that they may easily be removed. Milli-pedes burrow into these traps, and thus may be collected, extracted and destroyed.

Slugs

Slugs feed above the ground during the night and below ground at any time. Their eggs are white, translucent and glistening, and may be the size of a little bead, or tiny pearl. When digging, destroy any eggs found.

Control Measures. Make up a bran and Paris Green bait as advised for surface caterpillars.

Another good method is to mix a saltspoonful of powdered Metaldehyde fuel with a handful of bran or bread crumbs and place small heaps of this bait at 4-foot distances along the rows of cloches. The slugs will leave any crop for this bait, and will be killed in large quantities.

When digging the land in autumn or winter, incorporate a mixture of finely divided copper sulphate and hydrated lime, mixed in equal parts. This should be used at the rate of 1 ounce to the square yard. This mixture will kill any slug that touches it in the winter.

Wireworms

Make holes 2 feet apart and 8 inches deep with a walking stick, drop a piece of Paradichlorbenzene into the bottom of each -the size of a French bean. Stamp down to close the hole immediately afterwards. Fork in non-tainting Gammexane at the rate of 1 ounce to the square yard.

Cabbage Root Maggot

See Mercuric Chloride treatment as for Club Root, or dust around the plants at planting time with Calomel Dust.

DISEASES

Club Root

Club root is sometimes called " finger and toe ", or " anbury ". The roots will be found to be swollen and be turned into a club-like mass. If opened they will be found to be very evil smelling.

Control Measures. Before sowing the seed, water the seed-beds with a solution of mercuric chloride, diluting 1 ounce in 12 gallons of water. Fourteen days afterwards see that the seedlings are watered again with a similar solution. When planting out any members of the cruciferæ family (*i.e.*, cabbages, cauliflowers, sprouts, wallflowers, Virginian stock, swedes, turnips, etc.), ¼ pint of a similar solution should be poured into each hole.

Those who do not care to use this poisonous chemical may use Brassisan on the seed-bed at the rate of 1 ounce per square yard, sprinkling the dust over the soil evenly.   This product may also be applied in the dibble holes at planting time.

Botrytis

This is a fungus disease, which mainly attacks lettuces and is usually at its worst in the autumn and winter, when the light intensity is reduced and damp conditions prevail.   The plants rot off at the base, and brown mouldy patches appear on the leaves.

Control Measures.   It is most important never to allow seedlings to overcrowd.   Keep the leaves of the plants as dry as possible.   Dust with Folosan dust directly the trouble is seen.

Lettuce Mildew

There are two kinds of mildew—powdery mildew and downy mildew.   Both appear on the undersides of the leaves.   The white fungus will be seen, and the leaves will then turn yellow and decay.

Control Measures.   Never allow overcrowding.   See that there is plenty of potash in the soil, which ensures firm leaves. These are less liable to attack.

Dust the plants with sulphur dust immediately the trouble is noticed.

PESTS AND DISEASES OF FRUITS

As this book deals only with strawberries, raspberries, peaches and vines, the pests and diseases referred to are the ones which attack those crops, including only those which affect cloche users.

RASPBERRIES

Aphides

These may cause curled leaves or stunted shoots, and it is possible also that they cause the transmission of virus diseases.

Control Measures.   Spray the canes in December with a good tar distillate wash, using a 5 per cent. solution.   In summer spray with liquid Derris if aphides appear.

Raspberry Beetle

This beetle appears in May and lays eggs in the flowers. These hatch out into small white grubs which malform the fruits and cause them to be " maggoty ".

Control Measures. It is seldom that beetles get under cloches, but if there is any sign of them spray immediately with Derris and a detergent like Shellestol or dust with Derris powder.

STRAWBERRIES

Aphides

These attack the leaves and flow of sap. They are carriers of virus diseases and may also cause curled leaves.

Control Measures. Spray with nicotine and soft soap—formula : $\frac{1}{4}$ ounce nicotine and $\frac{1}{4}$ pound soft soap to $2\frac{1}{2}$ gallons of water. Spray the crowns of the plants and cover the undersides of the leaves also about the second week of April, and again early in May. Burn the straw used to litter the beds in order to kill the aphides on the old leaves.

Before planting " maidens "—*i.e.*, one-year-old plants—immerse them in warm water at exactly 110 degrees F. for twenty minutes. This will kill all pests present on the young plants.

Other pests that may attack strawberries are leather-jackets, slugs, snails, the larvæ of the chafer beetle, etc., and the control of these will be found at the beginning of this chapter.

PEACHES

Peach Leaf Curl

The symptoms are the curling up of the leaves which turn pinky red in the latter stages and finally these leaves may fall to the ground and cause serious defoliation. The spores of the fungus winter in the bud scales and these spores attack the young leaves directly they open.

Control Measures. Spray the trees just before the buds begin to swell towards the beginning of February with colloidal copper solution, using a wash such as Bouisol.   In very severe attacks, give an autumn application after the leaves have fallen.

VINES

Powdery Mildew

White powdery patches appear on the leaves, sometimes these spread to the fruits, causing them to crack.

Control Measures.   Dust with a fine sulphur dust directly the powdery patches are seen.   As an alternative, spray with a colloidal sulphur wash such as Sulsol.   Water the ground because the disease is always far worse when the soil is really dry.

SOWING AND CROPPING GUIDE

The Chart below shows when each crop should normally be sown and when it may be picked under ordinary climatic conditions.

Crop	Sow in South	Sow in North	When ready
Broad Beans .	Mid-Jan.	Early Feb.	May
Dwarf Beans .	Mid-March	Early April	June
Runner Beans .	Early April	Late April	July
Beetroot . .	Late Feb.	End of March	June
Spring Cabbage	Mid-Oct.	Late Sept.	March
Summer Cabbage . .	Late Jan.	Late Feb.	May
Carrots . . .	Mid-Jan.	Mid-Feb.	May
Lettuces . .	Mid-Aug.	Late July	Nov.–Dec.
Lettuces . .	Mid-Sept.	—	Jan.–Feb.
Lettuces . .	Mid-Oct.	Late Sept.	April
Marrows (plant out) .	Mid-April	Early May	June
Onions . . .	Mid-Jan.	Early Feb.	Sept.
Peas. . . .	Mid-Jan.	Mid-Feb.	May
Radish . . .	Early Jan.	Early Feb.	March
Spinach. . .	Early Oct.	Late Sept.	Nov. to March
Turnips . . .	Mid-March	Early April	May
Tomatoes (plant out) .	Late March	Mid-April	July, Aug.

Northern results are always interesting. Those given below are from Royston, Nr. Barnsley, Yorks.

Sowing or planting date	Subject	Cloches off	Cloche grown, first picking	Open grown, first picking	Advance, days
Mar. 1	Mint . . .	Mar. 29	Mar. 30	April 10	11
Mar. 29	Peas. . . .	May 5	June 19	July 10	21
Mar. 29	Lettuce . . .	May 17	May 17	June 12	26
Mar. 29	French Beans .	June 7	June 19	July 24	35
June 7	Marrows . .	July 12	July 17	Aug. 7	21

THE CLOCHE HANDLE AND PANEL

This invention allows any type of barn cloche to be given roof ventilation and further, it allows a roof glass to be removed entirely, thus making it unnecessary to move the cloche when working at the crop underneath.

You can imagine what a difference this will make when growing a crop of frame cucumbers or melons, where the plants have to be stopped and, in the case of melons, the flowers have to be pollinated. Each cloche in the row had to be moved and put back carefully in exactly the right alignment. With the new design, cloches need never be moved, except from crop to crop. Once placed carefully in position they will remain where they are until it is time to move them to the next crop in the rotation. Think what this will mean in the winter, when violets or polyanthus have to be picked from under the cloches. Sometimes the cloches get frozen to the ground, and it is impossible to lift them. Now it is possible to pick flowers from underneath whatever the conditions outside.

The job of taking out a roof glass and replacing it is perfectly simple, quick and safe. The new V handle is so shaped that the sheet falls naturally into position, and when it is removed the H panel keeps the cloche rigid, because the panel actually does the work of the sheet of glass which has been taken away. The rest of the design of the cloche remains unchanged. It is just as stable, simple to erect and resistant to wind as the old pattern. Glass, base wires and eaves wires are exactly the same as before, and the old type of barn cloche can be converted into the new type simply by buying the new V handle and H panel. There are two different sizes of panels, 12 inches

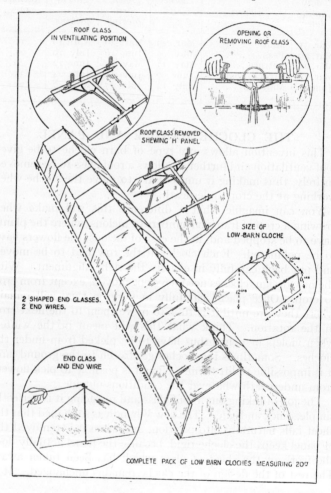

ROOF GLASS
IN VENTILATING POSITION

OPENING OR
REMOVING ROOF GLASS

ROOF GLASS REMOVED
SHEWING 'H' PANEL

SIZE OF
LOW BARN CLOCHE

2 SHAPED END GLASSES.
2 END WIRES.

END GLASS
AND END WIRE

COMPLETE PACK OF LOW BARN CLOCHES MEASURING 20"

and 9 inches, the first to convert a cloche with a 12-inch roof like a large barn or a low barn, the second for a cloche with a 9-inch roof like a long barn.

The handles are exactly the same for all types of barn cloches, and they will in future also be fitted to tent cloches, as they allow ventilation to be given at the ridge.   H panels cannot be used with the old type of handle, but must be used with the V handle.

In the past when extra ventilation was required for the crops under cloches the usual procedure was to space them out, so that they stood a few inches apart.   This was quite effective, though slightly laborious, but it had one or two disadvantages. In the first place, if the space was too wide birds were admitted. In the second place, the ventilation was from top to bottom, whereas horticulturally it is far better to give it in the roof. The other method of giving extra ventilation, *i.e.*, removing the ends of the rows, is to be deprecated because it causes dangerous draughts.   The new V handle enables top ventilation to be given to each cloche.   The glass slides easily into the ventilating notch, and the cloche remains perfectly rigid.   It is not suggested that the cloches should be opened and closed every day.   This is quite unnecessary.   When a hot spell comes along all the cloches can be given top ventilation, or, if preferred, every third or fourth cloche, just as in a greenhouse one opens ventilators at intervals along the top of the roof. The job is simple and quick, and, still more important, absolutely effective.   As a rule, most crops would do better with a small amount of top ventilation from May onwards except in cold districts or during cold spells of weather.   Tent and barn cloches can both be ventilated in this way.

SOWING AND GROWING VEGETABLES UNDER CLOCHES

Note.—The Earliest times of sowing are in ordinary print
and the Latest times in italics

Vegetable	South	Midlands	Scotland	Type of Cloche
Beetroot	End February *Mid-April*	Beg. March *Beg. May*	Mid-March *Mid-May*	Barn
Beans (Broad)	Mid-Jan. *End March*	End Jan. *Beg. April*	Beg. Feb. *Mid-April*	Large Barn or Tomato " T "
Beans (Dwarf)	Mid-March *End April*	End March *Beg. May*	Beg. April *End May*	Large Barn
Haricot Beans	Mid-March *End April*	End March *Beg. May*	Beg. April *End May*	Large Barn
Runner Beans	Beg. April *Beg. May*	Mid-April *Mid-May*	End April *End May*	Large Barn or Tomato " T "
Broccoli	Beg. March *Beg. April*	Mid-March *Mid-April*	End March *End April*	Any
Brussels Sprouts	End Jan.–Feb. *End March*	Mid-Feb.–March *Beg. April*	End Feb.–March *Mid-April*	Any
Cabbage, Summer Spring	End January *Beg. March* Mid-October *Mid-November*	Beg. February *Mid-March* Beg. October *Beg. November*	Beg. February *End March* End September *October*	Small Tent or Barn

156

	Mid-January *Beg. April*	End January *Mid-April*	February *End April*	
Carrots	Mid-January *Beg. April*	End January *Mid-April*	February *End April*	Barn
Capsicum	Mid-April *Mid-May*	End April *End May*	Beg. May *Beg. June*	Barn
Cauliflower, Spring Autumn	Jan.–Feb. *Beg. April* End Sept.–Oct. *End October*	End Jan.–Feb. *Mid-April* Mid Sept.–Oct. *Mid-October*	Feb.–March *End April* Beg. Sept. *End September*	Any
Celeriac	Mid-February *End March*	Early March *Beg. April*	End March *End April*	Any
Celery	Mid-February *End March*	Early March *Beg. April*	End March *End April*	Any
Coleworts	April–July *Beg. April*	Mid-April–July *Mid-April*	May–Early July *End April*	Earn
Corn Salad	June–Mid-Sept. *Mid-September*	June–Beg. Sept. *Beg. September*	June–End July	Earn or Large Tent
Cress and Mustard	Almost any time	Almost any time	Almost any time	Any
Cucumbers	Mid-April *Mid-May*	End April *End May*	Beg. May *Beg. June*	Large Barn or "T"
Egg Plant	Mid-April *Mid-May*	End April *End May*	Beg. April *Beg. June*	Barn or "T"

SOWING AND GROWING VEGETABLES UNDER CLOCHES—continued

Vegetable	South	Midlands	Scotland	Type of Cloche
Endive	June–September	June–End August	June–Early August	Barn or Large Tent
Kale	Late Feb., Early March, *Beg. April*	Mid-March *Mid-April*	End March, April *End April*	Barn
Kohl-Rabi	Early March *Beg. April*	Mid-March *Mid-April*	End March *End April*	Barn
Leeks	Jan.–Feb. *Beg. April*	End Jan.–Feb. *Mid-April*	Feb.–March *End April*	Tent or Barn
Lettuce, Spring / Winter	Jan.–Feb. *Beg. April* / Mid-Aug., Mid-Oct. *October*	End Jan.–End Feb. *Mid-April* / Beg. Aug., Beg. Oct. *October*	Beg. Mar.–End Mar. *End April* / End July, End Sept. *September*	Barn or Tent
Marrow	Mid-April *Mid-May*	End April *End May*	Beg. May *Beg. June*	Any
Onions, Spring / Harvest	Mid-August / Mid-Jan.–Mid-Mar.	Early August / End Jan.–End Mar.	End July / Beg. Feb.–Beg. Apr.	Barn
Parsley	Early March *Early April* / Early August *Mid-August*	Mid-March *Mid-April* / Late July *End July*	Late March *End April* / Early July *Mid-July*	Tent or Barn
Parsnip	February *End March*	Early March *Beg. April*	Mid-March *End April*	Tent or Barn

	Mid-January *End April* Any month following till August	End January *Beg. May*	Mid-February *End May*	Barn or Tomato "T"
Peas				
Peas, Asparagus	Early March *End April*	Mid-March *Beg. May*	Late March *End May*	Barn
Peas, Sugar	Jan.–May *End April*	Beg. Feb.–May *Beg. May*	End Feb.–June *End May*	Large Tent or Barn
Potatoes	Mid-February *End April*	End February *Beg. May*	Early March *End May*	Barn or Large Tent
Radish	Jan.–April *End March*	End Jan.–April *Beg. April*	Early Feb.–May *End April*	Any
Salsify	Early April *End April*	Mid-April *Beg. May*	End April *Mid-May*	Large Tent or Low Barn
Savoys	As Kale			Any
Spinach, New Zealand	April *Mid-May*	End April *End May*	May *Beg. June*	Barn or Large Tent
Spinach (Perpetual)	March–August *End April*	Beg. April Beg. Aug. *Beg. May*	End April End July *End May*	Barn
Spinach, Seakale	Ditto	Ditto	Ditto	Barn or "T"

SOWING AND GROWING VEGETABLES UNDER CLOCHES—continued

Vegetable	South	Midlands	Scotland	Type of Cloche
Spinach, Prickly or Winter	Oct.–Feb. *End Oct., End Mar.*	October–March *Mid-Oct., Beg. Apr.*	September–April *Mid-Sept., End Apr.*	Tent or Barn
Sweet Corn	End March *Beg. May*	Beg. April *Mid-May*	Mid-April *End May*	Barn or Tomato " T "
Tomato	End March	Beg. April	Mid-April	Tomato " T " or Barn
Turnip	Beg. February *End August*	End February *Beg. August*	Beg. March *July*	Tent or Barn

CLOCHE SOWINGS FOR THE FIRST FOUR MONTHS OF THE YEAR

	January and February			February and March			March and April		
	South	Midlands	North	South	Midlands	North	South	Midlands	North
Broad Beans	Mid-Jan.	Late Jan.	Early Feb.	*	Early March	Early Feb.	†	Early March	Late March
Beetroot	Late Feb	Not yet	Not yet	Late Feb.	Mid-Feb.	Late March	—	—	—
Brussels Sprouts	Late Jan.	Mid-Feb.	Late Feb.	*	*	Late Feb.	—	—	—
Cabbage (Summer)	Late Jan.	Early Feb.	Late Feb.	*	Mid-Feb.	Late Feb.	—	—	—
Carrots	Mid-Jan.	Late Jan.	Mid-Feb.	*	*	Mid-Feb.	—	Early March	Late March
Cauliflowers	Mid-Jan.	Late Jan.	Early Feb.	*	*	Early Feb.	†	Late April	Not yet
Celery (White)	Mid-Feb.	Not yet	Not yet	Mid-Feb.	Early March	Late March	†	Late April	Not yet
Cucumbers	—	—	—	—	—	—	Mid-April	Late March	Early April
Egg Plant	—	—	—	—	—	—	Mid-April	Late April	†
French Beans	—	—	—	—	—	—	Mid-March	Late March	†
Leeks	Early Jan.	Late Jan.	Mid-Feb.	*	Mid-Feb.	Mid-Feb.	†	Late April	Not yet
Lettuce	Mid-Jan.	Mid-Feb.	Mid-Feb.	*	*	Mid-Feb.	Mid-April	Late April	Not yet
Marrows	—	—	—	*	—	—	Mid-April	Late April	†
Melons	—	—	—	*	—	—	Mid-April	Late April	†
Onions	Late Jan.	Late Jan.	Early Feb.	*	*	Early Feb.	Early March	Mid-March	Late March
Parsley	—	—	—	*	*	Early Feb.	Early March	Mid-March	†
Peas	Mid-Jan.	Late Jan.	Early Feb.	Mid-Feb.	Late Feb.	Early Feb.	Early March	†	Early March
Potatoes	Mid-Feb.	Late Feb.	Not yet	*	*	Early March	†	†	†
Radish	Early Jan.	Late Jan.	Early Feb.	*	*	Early Feb.	Early April	Mid-April	Late April
Runner Beans	Any time	Not yet	Not yet	—	—	—	†	March	April
Spinach (Prickly)	—	—	—	*	March	Not yet	Early April	Mid-April	Late April
Sweet Corn	—	—	—	—	—	—	Late March	Early April	Mid-April
Tomatoes	—	—	—	—	—	—	Mid-March	Early April	Early April
Turnips	—	—	—	*	*	Not yet	—	Early April	Early April

* Earliest sowings recommended in January, but successional cloche sowings may still be made.
† Earliest sowings recommended in January or February, but successional cloche sowings may still be made.

SOME "PAYING" CLOCHE VEGETABLE CROPS

Crop	Varieties suggested	Months under cloches	Months in open	Remarks
Brussels Sprouts plants	Cambridge No. 5	Jan. to March	April	
Cabbage plants	Clucas 218	Jan. to March	April	
Onion plants		Jan. to March	April	Transplanted from October sowing
Lettuce	May King	Jan. to March	April	In succession
Radishes	Sparkler 50-50 / Scarlet Globe	Jan. to April		
Broad Beans	Aquadulce	Jan. to April	May	
Carrots	Early Nantes / Delicatesse	Jan. to April	May	
Peas	Laxton's Superb	Jan. to April	April and May	
Cauliflower plants		Feb. to April		
Leek plants	Musselburgh	Feb. and March	April and May	
Turnips	White Milan	March and April	May	
Beet	Crimson Globe	March and April	May	
Strawberries	Royal Sovereign	March to May	June to Feb.	
French Beans	Masterpiece / The Prince	March to May	June and July	
Peas	Foremost	April	May and June	
Lettuce	Unrivalled	April	May and June	
Tomato plants	Various	April and May	June to Aug.	Transplanted or sown in situ
Marrows (Bush)	"	April and May		Transplanted
Tomatoes	Any early variety	April and May	June to Aug.	

Crop	Variety			
Runner Beans	Princeps	April and May	June to Sept.	
Sweet Corn	{ John Innes, Kendall's Giant }	May	June to Sept.	
Cucumber and Marrow plants				Transplanted or sown *in situ*
Cucumbers	{ Perfection, Wither's Prize, Ridge }	May and June	July to Aug.	Transplanted
Melons	Cantaloupe	May to Sept.	July and Aug.	Transplanted
Tomatoes	Woodward's Open Air	June, Sept. and October		Transplanted
Cucumbers	Hampshire Giant	June and July	Aug. and Sept.	May be sown *in situ*
Onion Sets		June to Aug.	May	Cloche after germination
French Beans	The Prince	Sept. to Nov.	July and Aug.	Sown in open
Endive	Batavian	Sept. to Nov.	July and Aug.	Sown in open
Spring Onions		Oct. to March	Aug. and Sept.	Sown in open
Mint		Oct. to March	Rest of year	Cloche second year
Parsley	Myatt's Garnishing	Oct. to March	Aug. and Sept., April and May	Sown in open
Lettuce	Imperial	Oct. to Dec.		To transplant in Dec. or Jan.
Lettuce plants	May King	Oct. to March	April	
Cauliflower plants	Early Bird	Oct. to April	Aug. and Sept.	Sown in open
Peas	Early Bird	Nov. to March	April to May	

N.B.—This table refers to the Southern Counties—for Northern and colder districts it may be necessary to keep the crops covered later in the spring and earlier in the autumn.

RESULTS FROM LOW BARN CLOCHES IN LANCASHIRE

Crop	Variety	Length of cloched rows, yards	Sown	Transplanted	Cloched	De-cloched	Picking		Quantity
							First	Last	
Lettuce	May Queen	120	Oct. 9	Feb. 5	Feb. 5	April 27	April 27	May 5	86 doz.
,,	Clucas Winter Crop	120	Oct. 9	Feb. 5	Feb. 5	April 27	April 27	May 9	79 doz.
Peas	Meteor	240	Feb. 5	—	Feb. 5	April 27	June 9	June 14	546 lb.
Tomatoes	Stonor's Dwarf Gem	100	Mar. 13	May 1	May 1	June 6	July 24	Sept. 7	450 lb.
,,	Potentate	85	Mar. 13	May 1	May 1	June 6	Aug. 16	Sept. 7	365 lb.
,,	Clucas 99	35	Mar. 13	May 1	May 1	June 6	Aug. 16	Sept. 15	110 lb.
,,	Stonor's Outdoor	35	Mar. 13	May 1	May 1	June 6	Aug. 7	Sept. 7	150 lb.
Cucumber	Hampshire Giant	110	May 9	June 7	June 7	July 18	Aug. 4	Sept. 13	1093 lb.
,,	Wither's Prize Ridge	140	May 9	June 7	June 7	July 18	July 20	Sept. 20	1548 lb.
Lettuce	Unrivalled	240	Aug. 20	Oct. 8	Oct. 8	—	Nov. 23	Dec. 5	136 doz.

Incidentally, the ground occupied was 750 square yards and the return was at the rate of over £1,200 per acre ! !

TYPICAL CLOCHED PEA RESULTS

County	Variety	Main crop (M) intercrop (I)	Sown	De-cloched	Picking		Lbs. per 100 yards of cloche
					First	Last	
Somerset	Kelvedon Wonder Foremost	M	Oct.–Nov. Jan.–Feb.	April 3	May	August	317
Norfolk	Meteor	M	Mid-Nov.	April 29	May 3	June 7	117
Surrey	Laxton Superb Kelvedon Wonder	I	Nov. 19	April 10	May 10	June 12	89
East Scotland	Economist Kelvedon Wonder	I	Mar.–April Mar. 15	May 15	June 15	July 14	162
Essex	Foremost	I	Feb. 8	Mar. 30	June 2	June 8	105
Isle of Wight	Onward	I	Feb. 14	April 27	June 15	July 13	223
Lancashire	Meteor	I	Feb. 5	April 27	June 19	July 14	228

TYPICAL RESULTS FROM CUCUMBERS UNDER CLOCHES

Station	Variety	Sown	Transplanted	Cloched	De-cloched	First pick	Last pick	Weight of crop in lbs. per yard
Caernarvonshire	Long Green	April 5 to May 9†	May 9 to 22	May 9 to 22	June 16 to 24	June 24	Sept. 8	30·60
Sussex	Outdoor	May 7†	June 7	June 7	Aug. 4	July 31	Oct. 9	10·85
Lancashire	Wither's Ridge	May 9†	June 7	June 7	July 18	July 20	Sept. 20	10·10
Isle of Wight	Bedfordshire Prize Ridge	June 1*	—	June 1	Aug. 2	Aug. 20	Oct. 2	8·78
Yorkshire	Best of All	—†	May 20	May 20	July 20	July 2	Sept. 15	7·65
Cambridge	Prize Ridge	April 9*	May 6	April 11‡	July 10	July 10	Sept. 6	9·13
East Lothian	Telegraph Butcher's Disease Resisting	—†	May 30	May 30	Sept. 16	Aug. 5	Sept. 16	6·07
Kent	Conqueror	April 10*	—	April 11‡	July 9	July 13	Sept. 10	8·32
Surrey	Hampshire Giant	April 9*	—	April 11‡	July 12	July 8	Sept. 15	15·21

* Sown under cloches.   † Sown in heated glasshouse.   ‡ Cloches over the ground to warm it.

BEDFORD TRIALS. BUSH VARIETIES OF TOMATOES

Variety	Type of cloche	Sown	Transplanted	Cloched	Picking		Lbs. per plant	Remarks
					First	Last		
Bison	Tomato	Jan. 31	April 27	April 27	July 25	Oct. 27	11·5	Not a particularly good variety
Victor	,,	,,	,,	,,	Aug. 3	Oct. 27	13·2	Not recommended
Stambovoi Alpapsev	,,	,,	,,	,,	July 17	Oct. 27	13·2	Vigorous and healthy
Stonor's Dwarf Gem	,,	,,	,,	,,	Aug. 4	Nov. 1	15·5	Excellent variety
Fargo	,,	,,	,,	,,	July 26	Nov. 6	13·3	Tendency to green shoulders on fruit
Rose Bush	,,	,,	,,	,,	Aug. 11	Nov. 7	11·0	Somewhat like Fargo

TIME-TABLE FOR LETTUCES

Sowing dates	Planting dates	Period cloched	Cutting time	Varieties
N. early Feb. / S. early Jan.	Feb., March	10 days before sowing till April	May and June	Imp. Trocadero / May King / Lobjoit's Green Cos
N. early Aug. / S. late Aug.	October	Nil	Early June	Arctic King / Winter Crop
N. 3rd week March / S. 1st week April	Thin out end April	10 days before sowing till mid-May	June–July	Borough Wonder / Lobjoit's Green Cos
N. Nil / S. Oct.–Nov.	Under cloches Nov.–Dec. In open early March	1 week before sowing until planted out	Mid to end June	May King / Attractie / Feltham King
N. early April / S. early March	Nil	Nil	July	All-the-Year-Round / Webb's Wonderful
N. mid-May / S. mid-May	Nil	Nil	End July, August	Webb's Wonderful / Continuity
N. mid-June / S. mid-June	Nil	Nil	End Aug., Sept.	Imp. Trocadero / Lobjoit's Green Cos
N. beg. to end June / S. beg. to end June	Nil	Sept.	End Sept., Oct.	May King / Imp. Trocadero
N. late July / S. mid-August	Early Sept.	Early Oct. to end Dec.	Oct. to end Dec.	Imp. Trocadero / May King
N. end September / S. early Oct.	Nov., Dec., Jan., Feb.	From sowing time to March or April	March, April, May	May King / Lobjoit's Green Cos

N.=North.   Nil = (under the heading " Planting dates ") no planting done.   The rows just thinned out.
S.=South.   Nil =;(under the heading " Period cloched ") cloches not used for this crop at all.

FLOWER CHART (SURREY TRIALS)

Flower	Sown	Transplanted	Cloched	De-cloched	First pick
Polyanthus	Plants bought	Oct. 2	Dec. 15	March 31	Feb. 20
Calendula	,,	Sept. 29	Nov. 15	March 31	March 4
,,	Sept. 26		Sept. 26	April 15	April 19
Myosotis	Sept. 28		Sept. 28	March 31	March 19
Larkspur	Sept. 28		Sept. 28	April 7	June 6
Sweet Sultan	Sept. 27		Sept. 27	April 7	April 27
Nigella	Sept. 30		Sept. 30	March 31	May 15
Cornflower	Oct. 6		Oct. 6	March 21	April 24
Godetia	Sept. 28		Sept. 28	March 21	June 8
Annual Scabious	Sept. 27		Sept. 27	April 20	June 25
Sweet Peas, cordons	Oct. 20		Oct. 20	March 30	May 19
Linaria	Sept. 26		Sept. 26	March 20	March 19
Viscaria	Sept. 30		Sept. 30	April 3	March 10
Gypsophila	Sept. 30		Sept. 30	April 3	May 8
Candytuft	Sept. 28		Sept. 28	March 30	May 23
Aster	March 8	April 27	March 8	June 13	June 30

FORTY YEARS YOUNG!

IN the year 1912, Major L. H. Chase invented the original Chase Continuous Cloche. The ensuing forty years have seen unceasing research and experiment with the determination to keep Chase Cloches ahead of all imitations and substitutes, in economy and horticultural perfection. *Over sixteen million are now in use.*

RIGID Chase cloches are light and portable yet completely rigid. They can be stacked on end on the few occasions when not in use.

EASILY VENTILATED The patent panel and handle enable these cloches to be ventilated at a touch and permit easy access to the crops by removing a top pane.

CORRECT WIDTH Wide enough to take 3 rows of lettuce, the largest cloche is narrow enough for water falling on the glass to seep to the roots of the plants. No lifting needed.

SLOPING ROOF Allows the rays of even the lowest winter sun to penetrate without being reflected and lost.

You can be SURE of

CONTINUOUS CLOCHES

Chase Catalogue sent free on request

CHASE CULTIVATION LTD., 2, CLOCHEHOUSE, SHEPPERTON

INDEX

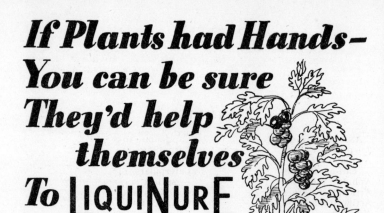